Better Homes and Gardens®

FRIENDSHIP QUILTING

BETTER HOMES AND GARDENS® BOOKS

Editor: Gerald M. Knox
Art Director: Ernest Shelton
Managing Editor: David A. Kirchner
Project Editors: James D. Blume, Marsha Jahns
Project Managers: Liz Anderson,
    Jennifer Speer Ramundt, Angela K. Renkoski

Crafts Editor: Sara Jane Treinen
Senior Crafts Editors: Beverly Rivers, Patricia Wilens
Associate Crafts Editor: Nancy Reames

Associate Art Directors: Neoma Thomas,
    Linda Ford Vermie, Randall Yontz
Assistant Art Directors: Lynda Haupert,
    Harijs Priekulis, Tom Wegner
Graphic Designers: Mary Schlueter Bendgen,
    Michael Burns, Mick Schnepf
Art Production: Director, John Berg;
    Associate, Joe Heuer;
    Office Manager, Michaela Lester

President, Book Group: Jeramy Lanigan
Vice President, Retail Marketing: Jamie L. Martin
Vice President, Administrative Services: Rick Rundall

BETTER HOMES AND GARDENS® MAGAZINE
President, Magazine Group: James A. Autry
Editorial Director: Doris Eby

MEREDITH CORPORATION OFFICERS
Chairman of the Executive Committee: E. T. Meredith III
Chairman of the Board: Robert A. Burnett
President and Chief Executive Officer: Jack D. Rehm

Friendship Quilting
Editor: Patricia Wilens
Project Manager: Jennifer Speer Ramundt
Graphic Designer: Harijs Priekulis
Contributing Graphic Designer: Patricia Konecny
Contributing Illustrator: Chris Neubauer
Contributing Copy Writer: Ciba Vaughan
Electronic Text Processor: Paula Forest

Cover project: See page 28.

CONTENTS

Circle of Friends
An Ongoing Tradition —————— 4

Before the advent of the camera and store-bought scrapbooks, memories of home, family, and friends were lovingly stitched into quilts. Here we tell the story of friendship quilting, a tradition continued by today's quilters. Organize a group project for friends or for a worthwhile cause. Our Friendship Basket quilt is a project made by one group to honor a friend.

The Block Party
Quilt Blocks to Make and Share ———— 12

If you're looking for a quilt pattern or a block design to contribute to a friend's quilt, here's a Spider Web scrap quilt plus eight different 9-inch blocks from which to choose. All are suitable for signatures.

Memories Everlasting
Making Friendships Last Forever ———— 24

We've gathered a charming gallery of six vintage quilts to inspire your own projects. Dating from the 1850s to the 1930s, these quilts immortalize the makers' affection in fabric and stitches. From a basic Album block set amid the intricacies of a Garden Maze, to the binding ties represented by the Friendship Knot, these quilts represent a variety of designs and techniques.

Hearts and Hands
Favorite Symbols to Make as Gifts ———— 44

The open hand of friendship and the loving heart are time-honored symbols of giving. Here are six gift ideas based on these favorite motifs. Perfect for youngsters or nonsewers is a "hands-on" wall hanging made with fusible webbing and fabric paint. Also included are a fancy Victorian pincushion, an appliquéd pillow, an elegant button pin, and a handy bookmark.

Celebrating Friendship
Quilting for Special Occasions ———— 58

A landmark in a friend's life is the perfect reason to collaborate on a friendship quilt. For the new bride, an expectant mother, a retiring leader, or a graduating student, here are five spectacular projects to commemorate an event with a lasting tribute.

Acknowledgments —————— 80

Circle of Friends

AN ONGOING TRADITION

"Within those stitches you will see and feel the special love and bond that is shared by a group of gals who quilt together."

Carolyn Edwards' words capture the centuries-old spirit that endures in the friendship quilts made by the Rather Bee Quilters of Des Moines, Iowa. After 12 years of making crib quilts for new babies, the Rather Bees are turning their needles to friendship quilts. One of the first completed is Marcia Shoemaker's basket quilt, *left*. As "quilter of the month," Marcia chose the pattern and fabrics; a month later, she had blocks from 20 friends. (See page 10 for instructions to make Marcia's quilt.) The Rather Bees' waiting list stretches through next year, and then they'll start all over again! The only rule is "don't make it too hard . . . we want to still be friends when this is over!"

Turn of the century photograph of quilting bee; courtesy of Glendora Hutson

FRIENDSHIP QUILTS: PIECES OF THE HEART

"Some folks has albums to put pictures in, some folks has a book and writes down the things that happen... but these quilts is my albums and diaries. I just spread out my quilts and it's like going back 50 or 60 years and living my life over again."
Eliza Calvert Hall, 1898

A friendship quilt, more than any other, preserves the tradition of fellowship that women have shared over the quilting frame for centuries. The memories and ties sewn into a friendship quilt far exceed its value as a bedcover.

Quilt making as a social activity

Nowhere has quiltmaking been more important in the lives of women than in the United States. In the early days of this nation, quilting parties defined the life-long arena of a woman's social life. Through girlhood, marriage, and raising a family, women who gathered to make quilts forged a bond of the joys and sorrows they held in common.

Glory of Baltimore Album Quilts

Fabric versions of autograph albums, friendship quilts were made in vast numbers between 1840 and the Civil War.

As an art form, the friendship quilt reached its height in the elaborately appliquéd album quilts made during this period in the mid-Atlantic states, particularly in and around Baltimore.

Often called Brides' quilts because they were frequently made by the friends of a prospective bride, the splendid floral appliqués of these quilts are evidence of the fine needlecrafts practiced by the well-to-do ladies of that time and place.

The pioneer's beloved keepsake

Often inscribed with sentimental verses of affection as well as names and dates, many friendship quilts were made by those who stayed in their comfortable, established towns. It was a fun, stylish thing to do, particularly for young girls. But friendship quilts took on a more poignant meaning for the pioneer.

The decades before the Civil War saw great change in America. The fabric of friends and family was strained, sometimes torn apart; women who followed hopeful husbands to the West never saw their eastern homes again.

In that time of slow communication over great distances, when good-byes too often were permanent, the friendship quilt became a lasting, treasured keepsake.

By carrying friendship quilts on the overland trails, women could bring a sense of their loved ones with them to brighten lonely

FRIENDSHIP QUILTS TODAY

days on the plains. Many such quilts made the long, dangerous trek westward to places like Ohio, Minnesota, Oregon, and California in the 1840s and 1850s.

The care with which so many of these quilts were preserved testifies to their heartfelt value. When other quilts served for everything from tents to shrouds, a friendship quilt was carefully tucked away as a precious heirloom.

The sentimental value of these quilts was given voice by Eliza Calvert Hall, author of *Aunt Jane of Kentucky*. This story of a colorful pioneer woman revolves around her quilts, making her an example of all the women who sewed deeply felt emotions into every stitch.

"There is a heap of comfort in making quilts, just to sit and sort over the pieces and call to mind that this piece or that is of the dress of a loved friend."

Family portraits

The friendship quilts from long ago now tell us much about the people who made them.

Many are family or community portraits. Some have only women's names on them, others include whole families, church groups, or the names of donors to a fund-raising campaign. These quilts helped many women face the pain of separation by allowing a departing recipient to take bits and pieces of her family with her.

The theme of family continued in friendship quilts through the Victorian period. Many Victorian friendship quilts include memorials to deceased family members. One such quilt made in Kentucky even features a family graveyard!

Commemorative ribbons sewn into the quilt were reminders of a family's accomplishments or participation in such events as fairs, reunions, or political campaigns.

A continuing tradition

Quilts made by groups or from scraps contributed by family and friends continue to be a treasured repository of memories, with each piece calling to mind fond recollections of the contributor.

 The 1990s scarcely seem analogous to the 1840s. After all, technology offers air travel and the telephone with which to easily maintain contacts. But friendship quilts still are made, and still fulfill the need to identify friends and community. Today's society is more transient than ever, and families moving from coast to coast often must leave friends and loved ones behind.

Records of our time

Today's friendship quilts continue the tradition of making a statement of community, family, and social commitment.

Perhaps the most notable example is the heartrending, ever-growing AIDS quilt. A banner-like block commemorates each victim of the disease, so that none is anonymous or forgotten.

Sadly, the quilt continues to grow—organizers of the nation-wide project vow to continue to honor the dead until a cure is found for the devastating virus.

Another renowned example of cooperation is the Boise Peace Project, which saw the combined efforts of women in Boise, Idaho, Great Britain, and the Soviet Union result in a quilt that celebrates the children of all nations.

On a smaller scale, for her friendship quilt, columnist Erma Bombeck collected signatures, messages, and doodles from 42 celebrities ranging from Walter Cronkite to Alan Alda.

"Remember me"

Quilters' groups and clubs have multiplied in recent years. More than ever before, quilters worldwide are coming together to share and to learn from one another.

Two such groups, the Rather Bee Quilters of Iowa and Minnesota's Quilters Along the Yellowstone Trail, are featured in this book (see pages 4 and 5 and 58 and 59). As Carolyn Edwards says, they are women who love to quilt together.

Today's friendship quilt affirms that "remember me" means as much now as it ever did.

Award-winning quiltmaker Judy Mathiesen, *left*, teaches a class on friendship fan quilts.

Classes bring today's quilters together to share ideas.

Innovative gadgets and sewing machines introduce new techniques to the '90s quilting bee.

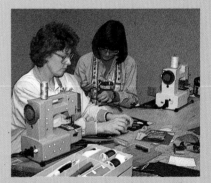

Carolyn Edwards, *right*, and Marcia Shoemaker work together to complete patchwork fans during Judy's class.

Circle of Friends

ORGANIZING A FRIENDSHIP PROJECT

Margot Cohen got the idea to make a "Homes for the Homeless" quilt after reading an article about homeless children. She organized 27 Long Island quilters who made personalized versions of a traditional house block and helped finish the quilt.

The grand result of this group effort, *below,* was auctioned to raise money for The Better Homes™ Foundation, a nonprofit organization that supports projects to help homeless families.

Sharing a common bond

Joining with others to create a friendship quilt is a wonderful way to show support and caring for another, to mark an important event, or to aid in healing in times of grief. It can be a means of raising funds or of expressing social concern.

The Long Island "Homes" quilt is a good example of this kind of cooperative effort. In addition to helping a good cause, the women who made it strengthened the bond between them by working together with a sense of fellowship. Also, they share the satisfaction of seeing their job well done.

Coordinating this kind of project is rewarding, but it's also hard work. Be prepared to commit a great deal of time, effort, and diplomacy to reach your goal.

Setting a realistic goal

There is no one plan that is guaranteed to succeed for every group. Sometimes the coordinators work alone or with very few others to formulate a plan for the project; in other cases, the group makes decisions as a committee.

Before selecting a design, assess the available time and talents of the quilting group, the preferences of the recipient, and the setting in which the finished quilt will be displayed. Setting reasonable goals and a realistic deadline will ensure a pleasant experience for all.

Choosing a design

The easiest type of friendship quilt to plan is one based on a block. For a sampler quilt, the decision-making can be no more than choosing the block size and a color scheme so that each person can make the block of her choice with her own fabrics.

If the profession or hobbies of the recipient makes a particular block appropriate, it can be made in a variety of fabrics for a single-block scrap quilt. An example of this is a pieced airplane block for a retiring airline pilot.

The "Homes" quilt is this kind of quilt—the repeated block emphasizes the theme of home, but it also allows each quilter to add personal touches so that no two houses are the same.

Appliquéd scenes of landmarks and historic events frequently are appropriate for community projects. Or, scenes of significant experiences can illustrate a "this is your life" type of quilt. In such cases, forming a small committee to consult and contribute design ideas is advisable.

When the guidelines and/or the patterns are worked out, it's time to enlist sewers.

Dividing up the work

In the initial enthusiasm, many people may volunteer to help. Be prepared that some may drop out, leaving others to shoulder an extra burden. Some volunteers will be able to contribute more than others. The larger the group, the more important it is to employ good management for everyone to be productive and satisfied.

The coordinator's foresight and diplomacy in assigning tasks is critical. Each person should be made to feel that she is making an important contribution. At the same time, a coordinator should take advantage of each person's strongest abilities.

If one person's sewing skills are weak, she can help prepare precut kits for others to sew; those with the best quilting stitches

might let others take charge of the piecing or the binding.

Be sure that no one plays so large a role that others feel left out or diminished. Also, you don't want an overtaxed worker to "burn out" before the job is done. A sensible balance of time and effort from all members is best.

Some groups have a recorder. Keeping a record of the quilt's evolution and those who take part in each stage could be the most fun job of all. A scrapbook of the quilt's development and the written thoughts of those who made it can be part of the gift.

A child's learning experience

Some of the most successful and popular friendship projects are those that involve children. The wide range of fabric paints and crayons available today make it easy for children to create their very own piece of a friendship quilt.

Many of these projects are coordinated by a teacher, parent, or scout leader who takes responsibility for obtaining materials and performing the more complicated tasks that are required.

In addition to teaching basic sewing skills, a children's friendship quilt is an ideal way to give youngsters a practical experience in cooperation and commitment.

Fund-raising

For almost 200 years, quilts have been a favorite tool of those seeking money for a good cause. An 1846 diary describes a church group that raised $200 for missionary work by selling signature space on a friendship quilt.

For years before the Civil War, raffles and fairs offering quilts for sale supported the abolitionist cause. Women's antislavery societies actually outnumbered the men's, and it was women who largely financed the movement with their fund-raising activities.

All kinds of civic, social, school, and church groups successfully use quilts as fund-raisers today.

For fund-raisers, the job of setting up a raffle or auction is so important that it should have its own coordinator and its own time

Long Island quilters Jeannine Love, Margot Cohen, and Janet Ratner *(left to right)* work on the quilt designed to raise funds for homeless families in the U.S.

schedule that begins long before the quilt is finished.

This coordinator is responsible for obtaining legal permits, getting the tickets printed and distributed, obtaining a site for the drawing or auction, and finding a suitable auctioneer or person to pick the winning ticket.

Publicity often is crucial to the success of such an event. This requires a fund-raising coordinator to handle such duties as getting posters printed and displayed or placing announcements in area newspapers. (It doesn't hurt to ask printers and newspapers to donate their services as a charitable contribution.)

There is plenty of work here for two people, who may contribute enthusiasm and public relations skills even if they are not quilters.

After the quilt is finished

Making the quilt isn't the end of the project—presenting it to the intended person or group is yet another goal to attain.

For a family or small group of friends, the presentation surely calls for a special celebration. A nonquilting friend can be party hostess to fulfill her contribution.

If the quilt is to hang in a public building such as a library or city hall, work with the appropriate officials to select a place for it to hang. Choose a spot where it is nicely displayed, but won't be exposed to deteriorating factors such as strong sunlight, which causes fading, or cigarette smoke, which will stain the fabrics.

Inscribe more than just a name

Friendship quilts deserve to be documented for posterity, so a lasting record of who made the quilt and for what reason should be an integral part of it.

If the quilt top does not offer suitable space, pen a brief account in indelible ink on muslin that can be sewn to the backing.

Along with the quilt, this will preserve a record of the loving and caring that created it.

Marcia's Friendship Basket Quilt

Shown on pages 4 and 5.

Finished quilt is approximately 70x85 inches. Finished basket block is 10⅝ inches square.

MATERIALS
5¾ yards of muslin fabric
½ yard of binding fabric
9x17-inch piece *each* of 20 different print fabrics for baskets and sawtooth border
5x11-inch piece *each* of 20 different print fabrics for "bows" and sawtooth border
5 yards of backing fabric
72x90-inch quilt batting
Rotary cutter and mat
Clear acrylic ruler
Pencil or fabric marker

INSTRUCTIONS
This quilt is made of 20 basket blocks set on the diagonal with alternating solid setting squares. Each basket is made from a different fabric, with a contrasting "bow" fabric at the top of the basket. The basket and bow fabrics also are used for the inner border and the outer sawtooth border.

There are 440 triangle-squares in the baskets and sawtooth border. Cutting and sewing these squares can be done traditionally, but our instructions describe a quick-piecing technique that eliminates templates and the cutting and sewing of 880 individual triangles. Read all instructions carefully to choose the method that you prefer.

CUTTING: The measurements given in these cutting directions include ¼-inch seam allowances. A rotary cutter is recommended for all cutting.

From an 8½-inch-wide section on one edge of the muslin, cut two 2⅛x82-inch borders and two 2⅛x64-inch borders.

Starting at the top of the cut edge of the muslin, measure and cut one piece 34x45 inches and a 34-inch square.

From the 45-inch-long muslin piece, cut 12 setting squares, each 11⅛ inches square. Cut the 34-inch square into four 16¼-inch squares. Cut each of these in half diagonally, then cut the resulting triangles in half diagonally again to obtain 16 triangles.

From the remaining muslin, cut one piece 35x42 inches and another 56x42 inches.

Cut two 8⅜-inch squares from one edge of the 35-inch-long piece. Cut each square in half diagonally to obtain the four corner setting triangles. From the remainder of this piece, cut twenty 5x11-inch pieces. Set these aside for the "bow" triangle-squares.

From the 56-inch muslin piece, cut twenty 8x14-inch pieces for the basket triangle-squares, cutting three 14-inch-wide segments across the width of the fabric.

Cut nine 2⅝x42-inch strips from the remaining muslin. From these strips, cut forty 2⅝x6⅞-inch A pieces and sixty-two 2⅝-inch B squares.

From each of the 20 block fabrics, cut one 8x14-inch piece for the triangle-squares. From the remainder, cut one B square. Save all the scraps for the inner border.

TRIANGLE-SQUARES: Referring to Figure 1, *above,* use fabric marker or pencil to draw a grid of 3-inch squares on the wrong side of an 8x14-inch muslin piece. Leaving a 1-inch border, first draw three 12-inch-long parallel lines 3 inches apart; complete the grid with horizontal lines to delineate eight squares. Draw diagonal lines through the squares as shown in Figure 2, *above.*

With the right sides together, match the marked muslin piece with one of the basket fabrics; pin together at the corners to prevent shifting. Machine-stitch ¼ inch from *both* sides of each diagonal line, as shown in Figure 3, *above.*

Cut the sewn triangle-squares apart by cutting directly on each *drawn* line. You will obtain 16 triangle-squares from each sewn grid; use 13 triangle-squares for each basket block and save three for the sawtooth border.

Mark and sew grids for 20 basket blocks; cut out all the triangle-squares.

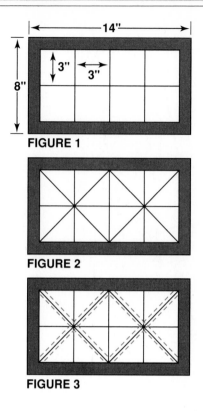

FIGURE 1

FIGURE 2

FIGURE 3

For the bows, mark each 5x11-inch muslin piece with one row of three 3-inch squares; draw a diagonal line through each square. Match the muslin with a bow fabric, then sew on both sides of the diagonal lines. Cut the six triangle-squares apart, saving two for each basket block and four for the sawtooth border.

If you prefer to cut and sew the triangles individually, mark each fabric in the manner described for the quick-piecing technique. Cutting the triangles apart on the drawn lines will result in 440 pairs of triangles ready to be sewn together by hand or by machine.

BLOCK ASSEMBLY: Refer to the block assembly diagrams, *opposite, top,* to make 20 basket blocks.

Join 13 triangle-squares and three B squares into four rows of four squares each, as diagramed. Note placement of the two triangle-squares of bow fabric. Press seam allowances to one side, alternating direction between rows.

The side bars of the block consist of a muslin A piece joined to a basket triangle-square. Sew one side bar to the left side of the block. To complete the block, sew

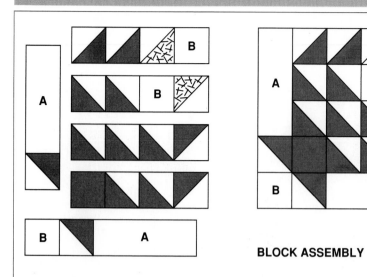

BLOCK ASSEMBLY

QUILT ASSEMBLY DIAGRAM

ing side unit, which is then sewn to the bottom of the block.

QUILT ASSEMBLY: Join basket blocks, plain squares, and all setting triangles into the diagonal rows indicated by red lines on the quilt assembly diagram, *below left.* Starting at the upper right corner, assemble rows.

BORDERS: Cut the print fabric scraps into 1¾-inch-wide pieces of random lengths. Add pieces of other coordinating fabrics if the quilt scraps are not enough to achieve the necessary lengths.

Sew two scrap strips 61 inches long; sew these to the top and bottom of the assembled quilt. Then make two strips 79 inches long and sew these to the sides.

The middle border is muslin. Sew 64-inch-long border strips to top and bottom; trim excess. Sew 82-inch-long strips to sides.

The sawtooth border uses the remaining 140 triangle-squares and two muslin B squares.

Join 40 of the triangle-squares together in a vertical row for each side border, always keeping the colored triangles on the bottom.

For the top and bottom borders, assemble four sets of 15 triangle-squares each. Join two of these sets for each border with a muslin B square between them.

Before sewing the top and bottom borders onto the quilt, compare the length of the border to the edge of the quilt. If any adjustments are necessary, you can replace the muslin B square with a muslin piece that is slightly larger or smaller as necessary.

Sew borders to top and bottom, then add side borders.

FINISHING: Divide the backing fabric into two 2½-yard lengths. Split one piece lengthwise and sew a narrow panel onto each side of the wide panel.

Layer the backing, batting, and quilt top; baste the three layers together. Quilt as desired.

See page 40 for tips on applying continuous binding.

BLOCK PARTY

QUILT BLOCKS TO MAKE AND SHARE

Part of the friendship quilting tradition is swapping bits of fabrics for scrap quilts and trading blocks for sampler quilts. This chapter features a scrap wall hanging, plus eight 9-inch patchwork blocks—all suitable for signatures—for you to make and share with your quilting circle. Some of the blocks are simple, others are more complex; all can be pieced by hand or by machine.

The Spider Web design, *left,* is a delightfully quick-to-piece variation on a very old theme— some versions of this pattern were popular as early as 1800.

Here, scrap fabrics create a kaleidoscope effect on a light background. The 5x6-inch Spider Web blocks are framed with a simple sashing and highlighted by tiny pieced setting squares. To get maximum use from our scraps, we saved the leftovers and made a colorful strip binding to frame the wall hanging.

Whether your scraps can extend to a wall hanging or a full-size quilt, the intricate design on the wide border will showcase your quilting stitches. Directions for quick-piecing the wall hanging begin on page 14 and include a full-size pattern for the border motif.

For a challenging make-and-trade block party, review the eight blocks on pages 16–23. Instructions and full-size patterns are included for each block.

Remember: a friendship block isn't finished until it's signed!

Spider Web Scrap Wall Hanging

Shown on pages 12 and 13.

The wall hanging measures 46½x47¼ inches. The finished Spider Web block is 5x6 inches.

MATERIALS
3¼ yards of muslin (includes backing)
Sixty 1¾x20-inch pieces of scrap fabrics
1⅜ yards of quilt batting
Rotary cutter and mat
Clear acrylic ruler
Nonpermanent fabric marker
Template material

INSTRUCTIONS
The pieced triangles in this wall quilt can be cut and sewn traditionally, but instructions are given for an easy, quick technique that enables you to cut all six pieced triangles for a block from one presewn pair of strips. Read all instructions before you decide which method is best for you.

All cutting instructions include ¼-inch seam allowances, unless stated otherwise. A rotary cutter is recommended for all cutting.

CUTTING: Cut a 15x42-inch muslin piece into eleven 1¼x42-inch strips. From these, cut thirty-five 6½-inch-long pieces and thirty-six 5½-inch-long pieces for the sashing.

Cut one each of the following strip widths down the full length of the remaining muslin: 4 inches, 13 inches, and 25 inches.

Cut the 25-inch-wide panel in half to make two 25x51-inch pieces for the backing.

From the 13-inch-wide piece, cut two 6½x50-inch borders and two 6½x37-inch borders.

From the 4-inch-wide piece, cut sixty 2¼x3⅝-inch rectangles; cut each rectangle in half *diagonally* to obtain 120 side triangles for the Spider Web blocks.

SPIDER WEB BLOCK: Sew two scrap fabrics together to make a 3x20-inch strip. Press the seam toward the darker fabric.

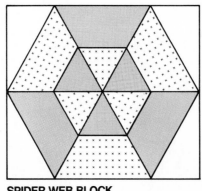

SPIDER WEB BLOCK

Make a template for the triangle pattern, *opposite*.

Refer to Figure 1, *below,* to cut six triangles from the sewn strip, adding a ¼-inch seam allowance around the template when cutting. Save all scraps of the sewn strips for sashing squares and binding. *Note:* If your ruler has lines marking a 60-degree angle, you can cut all the triangles with

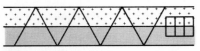

Figure 1

the ruler and rotary cutter, eliminating the template. With seam allowances added, the equilateral triangle has a 4-inch base.

Refer to the assembly diagram, *left,* to make one half-block; sew three triangles in a row, adding a muslin side triangle at both ends. Press seams to one side. Join two half-blocks at the center seam to complete the block.

Make 30 Spider Web blocks.

SASHING: From scraps of the sewn strips, cut 45 *pairs* of ⅞x1¼-inch strips for the sashing squares. Sewing along the length, stitch the two pieces of each pair together, checkerboard style.

Make a row of horizontal sashing by sewing five 6½-inch muslin sashing strips between six pieced squares. Make seven rows.

ASSEMBLY: Join Spider Web blocks into six horizontal rows of five blocks each, sewing a 5½-inch-long sashing strip between each block. Press the seam allowances toward the sashing.

BORDER QUILTING MOTIF

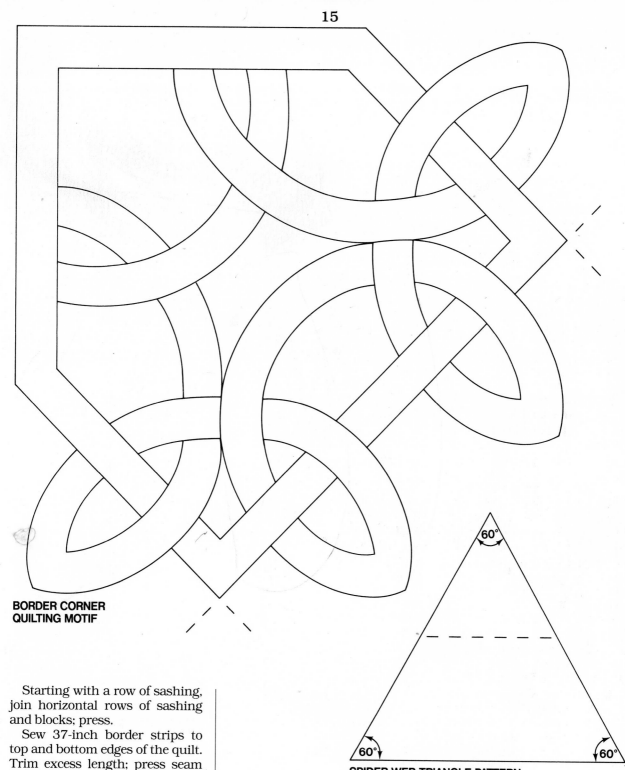

**BORDER CORNER
QUILTING MOTIF**

SPIDER WEB TRIANGLE PATTERN

Starting with a row of sashing, join horizontal rows of sashing and blocks; press.

Sew 37-inch border strips to top and bottom edges of the quilt. Trim excess length; press seam allowances toward borders. Add 50-inch side borders.

FINISHING: The border quilting design shown on the quilt on pages 12 and 13 is given here.

To mark this design on the finished quilt, begin by drawing a straight line on the border fabric ¼ inch outside the border seam line. Find the center of each border; mark four border motifs, *opposite*, on either side of the center point. Mark four connecting corner motifs, *above*, on each corner.

Seam backing fabric into one 50-inch length; press seam allowance to one side. Layer backing, batting, and quilt top; baste. Quilt as desired. Trim the batting and backing even with quilt top; remove basting and quilting marks.

From the remaining scrap fabrics, cut 1¼-inch-wide pieces up to 3 inches long. Selecting pieces at random, make four 1¼x48-inch binding strips. Press all the

seam allowances to one side, then press under a ¼-inch seam allowance on one long edge.

Matching the raw edge of the binding strip with the edge of the quilt, sew two strips to top and bottom edges through all layers. Turn pressed edge of binding over the quilt edge to the back; hand-sew the binding fold to the quilt backing. Repeat for side binding on the opposite two sides.

Patchwork blocks to make and share

Here's the perfect excuse to invite a group of friends over for a quilting social. We've selected eight great 9-inch blocks that are ideal for a friendship quilting project. Make one of each to give or trade.

Each block is suitable for hand or machine sewing and has a central space for signatures. Some blocks are more difficult to piece than others, so there's one that's just right for your skill level.

These blocks are presented on the next seven pages. A color photo, instructions, and assembly diagram are given for each block.

The patterns, A through Z, can be found *below* and on the following pages. Some patterns are used in more than one block; grain direction may vary in different blocks. All the patterns are the finished full-size, so be sure to add a ¼-inch seam allowance around each shape when marking and cutting fabrics.

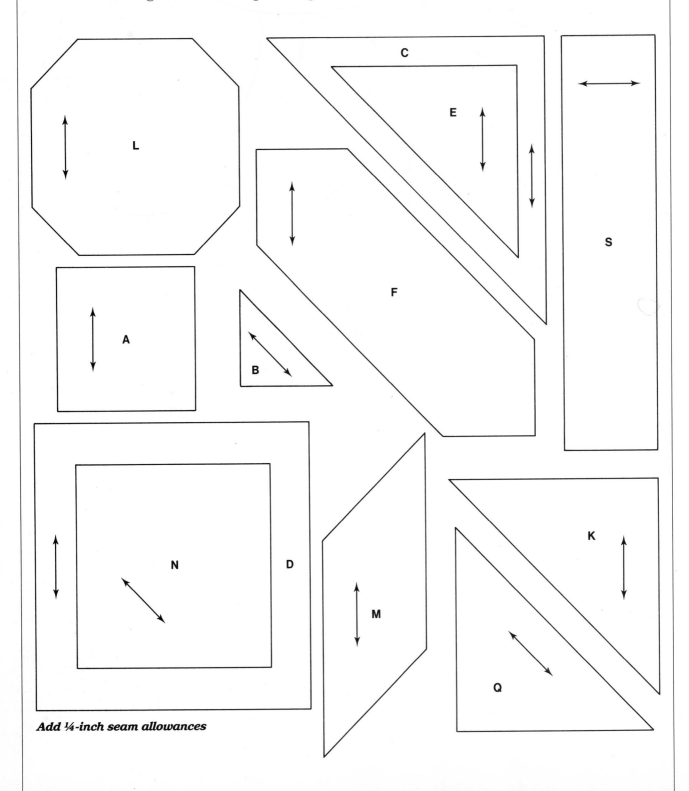

Add ¼-inch seam allowances

New Album Block

To make one block, cut eight of Pattern G and one of Pattern H from dark fabric; cut four of Pattern D from striped fabric. Cut four each of patterns A and C and two of Pattern G from print fabric.

For a corner unit, sew one dark G triangle onto adjacent sides of each A square as shown in the assembly diagram, *below*. Press seams toward the A square. Complete the corner unit by adding a C triangle; press the joining seam toward the solid triangle. Make three more corner units.

Make one center unit by sewing the two G print triangles onto the H piece.

Sew the four D squares and the five assembled 3-inch squares into three rows of three. Then join the rows, matching seam lines carefully; press seams toward the striped squares.

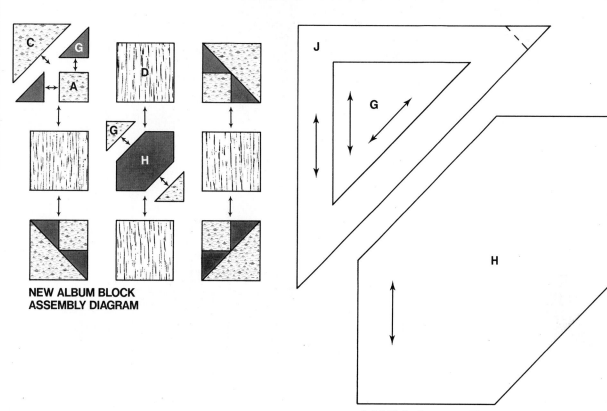

**NEW ALBUM BLOCK
ASSEMBLY DIAGRAM**

Add ¼-inch seam allowances

WCTU Patch

To make one block, cut eight of Pattern B and four each of patterns A and D from medium-value fabric; cut eight of Pattern B and two of Pattern E from dark fabric. Cut four of Pattern C from light print fabric and one of Pattern F from light solid fabric.

Sew light and dark B triangles into pairs as shown in the assembly diagram, *below left*. Sew the dark sides of these joined triangles onto adjacent sides of each A square, forming a larger triangle. Press seams toward the square.

Sew a C triangle onto the pieced triangle to complete the corner unit. Press this joining seam toward the C triangle. Make three more corner units.

To make the center unit, join an E triangle to each side of the F center piece.

Referring to assembly diagram, combine the five pieced squares with the four D squares. Sew the nine 3-inch squares together into three rows of three; join the rows, matching seam lines carefully.

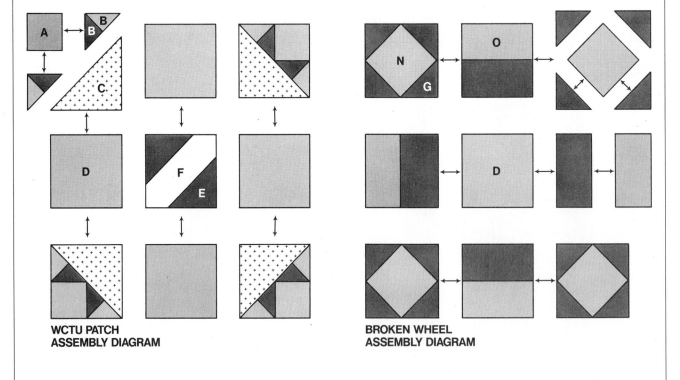

**WCTU PATCH
ASSEMBLY DIAGRAM**

**BROKEN WHEEL
ASSEMBLY DIAGRAM**

Patterns to make these blocks are on pages 16, 17, and 20.

Broken Wheel

To make one block, cut 16 of Pattern G and four of Pattern O from dark fabric. Cut one of Pattern D and four each of patterns N and O from light fabric.

Referring to the assembly diagram, *opposite,* sew G triangles onto each side of the N squares to make the four corner units. Sew light and dark O pieces together in pairs to make four side units.

Assemble pieced squares and the center D square into three rows as shown, then join rows.

Four Crowns

To make one block, cut one of Pattern D and 16 of Pattern G from dark fabric; cut four of Pattern C from medium-value fabric. Cut four of Pattern A and eight of patterns Q and G from print fabric.

Sew a Q triangle to each side of the D square; press seams away from center. Sew two C triangles onto opposite sides of the square as shown in the diagram, *below.*

Join light and dark G triangles to make eight triangle-squares. Sew a dark G triangle onto the light side of each square, then add a Q triangle to the row as shown.

Complete units as shown in the diagram, then join units.

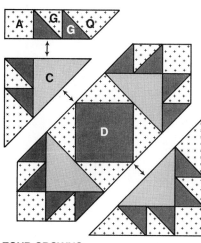

FOUR CROWNS ASSEMBLY DIAGRAM

Golgotha Block

Patterns for this block are *below* and on pages 16 and 17.

To make one block, cut four of Pattern P from striped fabric and four of Pattern Q from light solid fabric; cut eight each of patterns B and G from print fabric. Cut one of Pattern N, eight of Pattern B, and four each of patterns A and O from medium-value fabric.

Assemble top and bottom strips and the two side strips as shown in the assembly diagram, *below right,* using pieces A, B, G, and O.

Sew a Q triangle onto either side of two P pieces to make a large triangle; press the seams toward triangles. Sew remaining P pieces onto opposite sides of the N square; press seams toward center. Assemble center section by sewing a P-Q triangle onto opposite sides of the N-P unit.

Sew top and bottom strips onto the center section. Complete the block by joining side strips. Match the seam lines carefully.

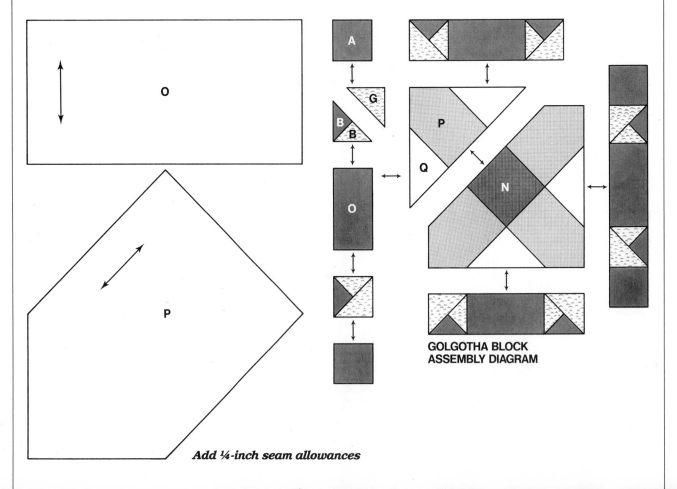

**GOLGOTHA BLOCK
ASSEMBLY DIAGRAM**

Add ¼-inch seam allowances

Triple Link Chain

Note: This block is one of the more difficult blocks shown.

Patterns for this block are on pages 16 and 17.

To make one block, cut one of Pattern L and eight of Pattern M from medium-value fabric; cut four of Pattern K and eight of Pattern J from print fabric. Cut four each of patterns G and K from light fabric.

Sew the J print triangles onto the center octagon (L), starting with a triangle on the longer right edge of the center octagon (indicated by an * on the assembly diagram, *below*). Sew only the top half of this seam, leaving the rest to be completed after the last triangle is added to the octagon. The edge created by this first seam gives you a straight line on which to sew the next triangle.

Continue adding triangles onto the octagon in a *counterclockwise* direction. Press each seam as you go, pressing away from the octagon. Keep the first triangle out of the way as you sew the last triangle onto the octagon; match the edge of the first triangle to the edge created by the last one and complete the seam down to the bottom edge.

Trim points off the four alternating J triangles as shown in the diagram. Make the assembled center unit into a square by adding four G triangles onto the trimmed side triangles as shown.

Make a corner unit by sewing two M pieces to either side of a light K triangle, then complete the unit with a dark K triangle. Make three more corner units.

Sew corner units onto center square, matching seam lines of the light K triangles in the corner units with the seam lines of the G triangles in the center square. Press seams toward corners.

**TRIPLE LINK CHAIN
ASSEMBLY DIAGRAM**

Friendship Links

Patterns for this block are *below* and on page 16.

To make one block, cut four each of patterns C, Q, and T, and one of Pattern N from print fabric; cut four of Pattern R and two of Pattern S from *each* link fabric.

Sew T pieces onto two R pieces of *each* fabric. With the T piece at the bottom of each unit, sew an R piece of matching fabric onto the left side of the unit, as shown in the assembly diagram, *below left*. Sew a Q triangle to the left edge of each unit. Complete each unit by sewing an S piece of contrasting fabric onto the bottom edge. Make four quarter-section units.

Match one edge of the N square with the edge of one quarter-section unit as shown. Starting at the matched edges, sew only half of this seam in order to create a straight edge for the next unit; the remainder of the seam is completed after the last unit is joined.

Sew around the square *clockwise,* adding second and third quarter-section units.

Add the last quarter-section to the edge formed by the third unit and the N square, holding the first unit away from this seam.

When the last unit is joined, you should have a straight edge to complete the first seam from the center N square to the edge.

Complete the block by adding C triangles at the corners.

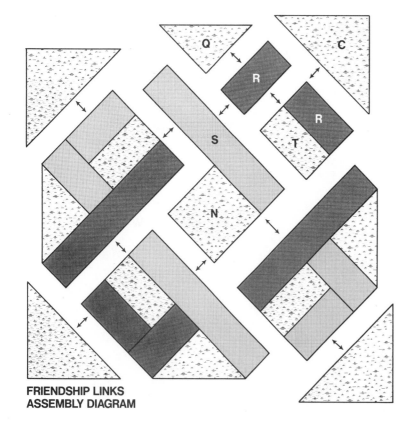

**FRIENDSHIP LINKS
ASSEMBLY DIAGRAM**

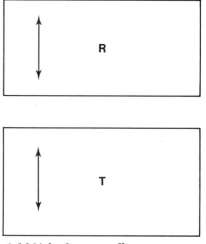

Add ¼-inch seam allowances

North Carolina Star

All of the patterns for this block are *below.*

To make one block, cut one of Pattern U and four each of patterns Z and W from light fabric; cut eight of Pattern W and four of Pattern V from dark fabric. Cut four of Pattern X and eight of Pattern Y from medium-value fabric.

Assemble four corner units by joining the W, X, and Y triangles as shown in the assembly diagram, *below.*

Sew a Z piece to either side of two V pieces as shown. Sew a V piece onto opposite sides of the U square. Assemble the center section by joining the V-Z units to the U-V unit.

Complete the block by setting the corner units into the center.

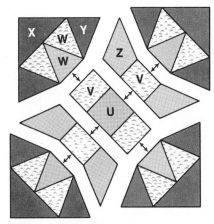

**NORTH CAROLINA STAR
ASSEMBLY DIAGRAM**

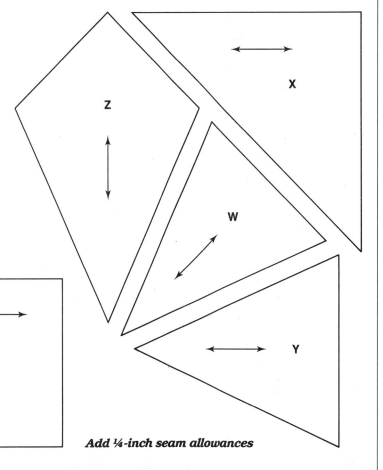

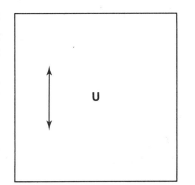

Add ¼-inch seam allowances

♦♦♦

MEMORIES EVERLASTING

FRIENDSHIPS LAST FOREVER

Many vintage friendship quilts survive in near pristine condition, protected by their sentimental value from the wear and tear of everyday use. All evoke deeply personal links to a gentler past, provide a touch of comfort in the present, and offer a tangible reminder that true friendship, as the poet Shelley said, is ever indeed "a refuge and a delight."

The Friendship Knot quilt, *left,* is a classic group project from the Depression Era. The quilt is undated, but the fabrics are typical of the 1920s and 1930s. This pattern, also known as Starry Crown and Friendship Wreath, was particularly popular during that period.

Though its origin is unknown, the quilt itself provides a few clues. First, it is undoubtedly a cooperative venture. The fabrics used for each of the 48 "knots" are all different, and each embroidered inscription is traced in a different hand. However, the quilting is remarkably consistent,

suggesting the quilt was assembled and quilted by a single hand.

To gather the blocks for this type of quilt, patterns often were distributed to friends and family members with a request that each make a block using remnants from a favorite dress.

Whatever the occasion that spurred the creation of this homey quilt—a marriage, or maybe a move to a new home—it surely was treasured as much as the friendships it celebrates and preserves.

Patterns and instructions for this quilt begin on page 32.

Perhaps the best loved and most frequently made friendship quilt pattern is the simple Album block, also known as the Chimney Sweep or Friendship block. Since the 1840s, in unlimited variation, the Album block has been the pattern of choice from Maine to California.

A superb example, our Album quilt, *right*, dates from the 1850s. In this version of the perennial favorite, 30 blocks—each made with a different calico—are set in a Garden Maze sashing, framed within a bold zigzag border.

Each block centers on a handwritten scrap of pious verse or flowery paean to friendship, followed by a signature and, sometimes, a date. Though the ink is faded, much is legible and the sentiments expressed still touch our hearts nearly 150 years later. For more about these inscriptions, see page 36.

The blue quilt, *below,* shows the same Album block in a simple diagonal set with alternating plain blocks.

The blocks, of which only two are signed, possibly were made in anticipation of a friendship project that failed to materialize. Later, as consolation perhaps, the quilter stitched them into this "everyday" quilt.

Patterns and directions for both Album block quilts begin on page 34.

Both of these quilts may be the work of single quiltmakers—one person's tribute to a roster of loved ones.

The Friendship Chain quilt, *above,* is dated 1931, Oklahoma. The inscriptions may have been solicited by mail rather than in person. In such cases, cut strips of fabric often were mailed to friends far and wide to be signed and returned posthaste. The quilter then could embroider the inscriptions at her leisure before piecing each cherished strip into a block.

The pattern for the embroidered quilt, *opposite,* is typical of many featured in needle arts magazines and kits of the 1930s and '40s.

A different name is embroidered on each 15-inch block, uniting nine friends with fabric and thread.

For patterns and instructions, turn to pages 38–41.

Despite wide-spread reliance on familiar designs, over the years imaginative quilters adapted a host of other patchwork patterns for friendship quilts. As long as space could be found for the requisite signature or inscription, almost any pattern might serve. The string-pieced star quilt, *left,* made in 1889, is a handsome case in point.

Thrifty 19th-century quiltmakers routinely saved and swapped even their slenderest scraps to stitch into such string-pieced designs.

"String piecing" defines the sewing together of narrow fabric strips to create yardage. From this new pieced material, pattern shapes, such as the diamonds for this eight-pointed star, can then be cut.

With a border, nine 24-inch-square star blocks combine to make a quilt 84 inches square. Signatures are embroidered on random strips of fabric.

A diversity of fabrics, a background fabric of rich green, and fine quilting lend this simple quilt an air of elegance that belies its humble scrap origins.

The pattern and step-by-step instructions for this quilt are on pages 42 and 43.

Friendship Knot Scrap Quilt

Shown on pages 24 and 25.

Finished quilt is approximately 66x88 inches. Each block is 11 inches square.

MATERIALS
7 yards of white fabric
⅛ yard *each,* or scraps, of 48 different print fabrics
⅝ yard of pink binding fabric
5½ yards of backing fabric
81x96-inch quilt batting
Light pencil or nonpermanent fabric marker
Embroidery floss to coordinate with fabrics
Cardboard or plastic template material

INSTRUCTIONS
The quilt pictured on pages 24 and 25 is made of 48 blocks arranged in eight rows of six blocks each. This block presents a real

piecing challenge—it has small pieces and curved seams and it requires setting in both single pieces and assembled units.

CUTTING: *Note:* The number of pieces to cut for a single block is listed first; the number of pieces needed for the entire quilt is shown in parentheses.

Make templates from patterns A–F, *opposite,* making a complete template for F, the center piece.

These patterns are finished size; add a ¼-inch seam allowance when marking and cutting. Mark grain lines on templates.

For each block, cut from the white fabric four *each* (192 each) of patterns B, C, C reversed, and E. Cut one (48) of Pattern F.

From the print fabric, for each block cut 16 (768) A diamonds and four (192) D pieces.

ASSEMBLY: Piece the A diamonds of each block to make four 4-diamond units. Pressing these seams open may be helpful before setting in the white pieces. Set in a B triangle in the center and the appropriate C pieces on each side of the diamond unit. Press these seams toward the darker fabric.

Combine each of the four D pieces with an E piece to make a corner unit. Clip the seam allowances so that the curved seam will lie flat. Press seams toward dark fabric.

Sew a corner unit onto each curved side of piece F, the center. Clip seam allowances; press seams toward dark fabric.

Set in the four-diamond units, carefully matching the seam lines of the side diamonds with the seam lines of the sewn D pieces.

Complete 48 Friendship Knot blocks.

Add penned or embroidered signatures in the center of each block. Names can be lightly written directly onto the cloth, or on paper first and then traced onto the fabric for embroidering.

Join the 48 completed blocks into eight horizontal rows, with six blocks in each row.

FINISHING: Cut backing fabric into two 2¾-yard lengths. Split one piece lengthwise and sew a narrow panel onto each side of the wide panel.

Layer the backing, batting, and quilt top; baste the three layers together. Quilt as desired.

When quilting is complete, trim batting and backing even with the quilt top. Bind the edges with straight or bias strips.

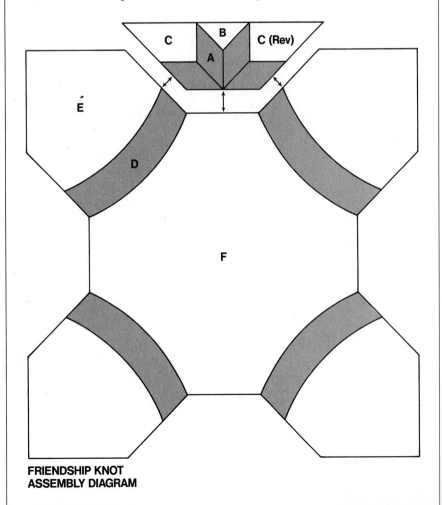

**FRIENDSHIP KNOT
ASSEMBLY DIAGRAM**

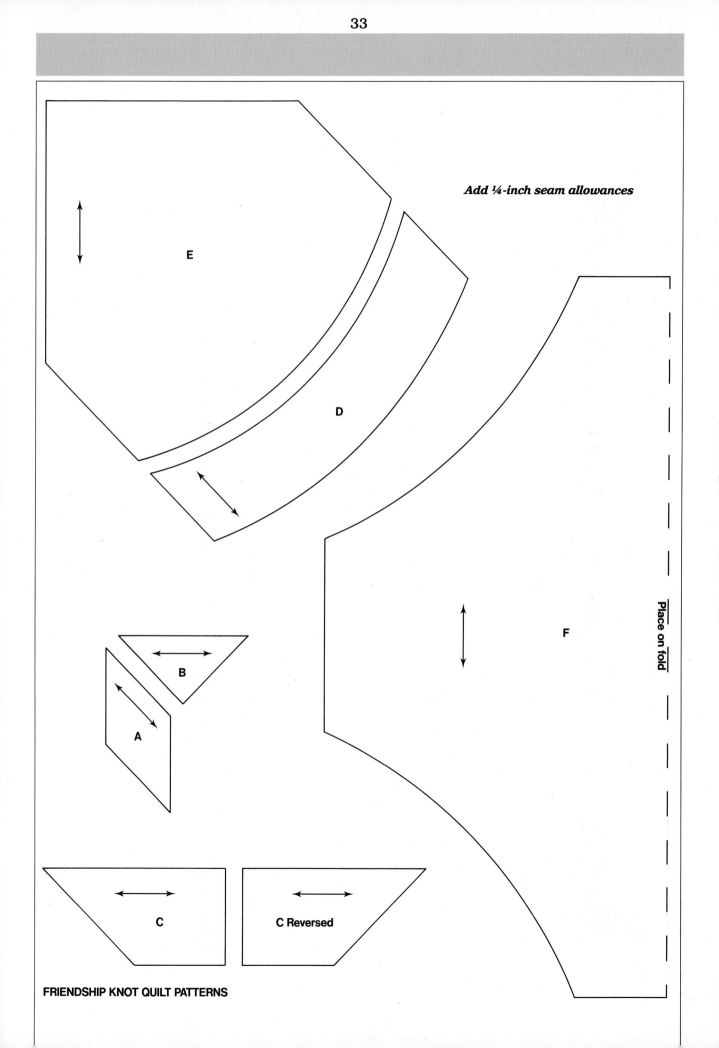

Add ¼-inch seam allowances

E

D

Place on fold

F

B

A

C

C Reversed

FRIENDSHIP KNOT QUILT PATTERNS

Garden Maze Album Block Quilt

Shown on pages 26 and 27.

Finished quilt is approximately 73x84 inches. A finished block is 9 inches square.

MATERIALS

4⅛ yards of muslin
3 yards of red print fabric (includes binding)
¾ yard of solid red fabric for zigzag border
⅛ yard *each,* or scraps, of 30 different print fabrics for Album blocks
5 yards of backing fabric
81x96-inch quilt batting
Template material
Rotary cutter and cutting mat
Heavy duty acrylic ruler

INSTRUCTIONS

This quilt is made of 30 blocks. The Garden Maze setting is made with a pieced sashing and a crisscross pieced sashing square. The zigzag border goes around only three sides of the quilt.

The block and sashing are easy to piece, but the crisscross sashing square requires cutting and piecing irregularly shaped pieces.

Instructions are given for strip-piecing the sashing.

CUTTING: Some of the pieces for this quilt are cut in the traditional manner, using templates and adding ¼-inch seam allowances; however, the setting strips for the Garden Maze are more easily cut using a rotary cutter. Instructions for cutting these strips include seam allowances.

Using the rotary cutter, cut one 3½x105-inch muslin strip and four 3½x96-inch muslin strips. From the red print, cut eight 1½x96-inch strips, two 3½x105-inch strips, four 1½x10½-inch strips, and eighteen 1½x9½-inch strips. Set all these strips aside for sashing.

Make templates for patterns A–H, *opposite.* Patterns are full-size; add seam allowances when marking and cutting fabric. Mark grain lines on each template.

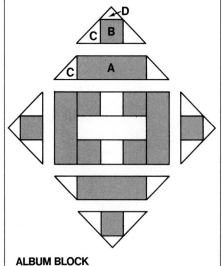

**ALBUM BLOCK
ASSEMBLY DIAGRAM**

Also from the muslin, cut the following pieces for the blocks (the requirement for one block is given first, the number needed for the entire quilt is shown in parentheses): one (30) A rectangle, two (60) B squares, 12 (360) C triangles, and four (120) D triangles.

From remaining muslin, cut 80 E triangles for the Garden Maze squares and 159 F triangles for the zigzag border.

Cut each scrap fabric into two 2⅛x42-inch strips. From each strip, cut four A and eight B pieces (adding seam allowances).

From the remaining red print fabric, cut 20 G and 40 H pieces for the Garden Maze squares. Marking the seam allowance on these pieces is helpful for the precise piecing that is required to set in the irregular shapes.

From solid red fabric, cut 161 F triangles for the zigzag border.

BLOCK ASSEMBLY: A signature can be added using an indelible ink pen after the block is sewn, or friends can personalize muslin A pieces before they are sewn into the blocks.

To construct an Album block, refer to the assembly diagram, *above left.*

Starting with the center unit, stitch a colored B square onto opposite sides of both muslin B squares; press the seams toward darker fabric. Sew these three-square strips onto the long sides of the muslin A rectangle; press seams toward center.

Stitch an A rectangle onto each side of the patchwork to complete the center unit as shown. Press seams toward colored A pieces.

Stitch a C triangle onto both ends of the remaining A pieces;

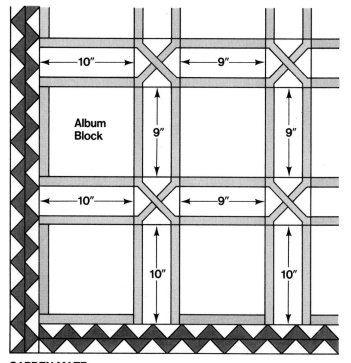

**GARDEN MAZE
ASSEMBLY DIAGRAM (SECTIONAL)**

press seams toward the dark fabric. Sew these units onto top and bottom of center unit as shown.

Sew C triangles onto opposite sides of the remaining B squares; press seams toward square. Complete four corner units by adding D triangles; press seams toward the triangle. Stitch corners onto block; press seams toward center.

GARDEN MAZE STRIPS AND SETTING SQUARES: Sew a red print sashing strip to both sides of the five muslin sashing strips. Press seams toward red fabric.

Use the rotary cutter to cut two of these strips into 18 segments, each 10½ inches long. Cut the remaining three strips into 31 segments, each 9½ inches long.

Use E, G, and H pieces to make 20 Garden Maze squares. Start by

sewing an E piece onto each side of the H pieces. Whether you are sewing by hand or by machine, stitch up to the angle; with the needle in the precise pivot point, turn the fabric to align the needle correctly and continue to sew. Press seams toward red fabric.

Use the same procedure to sew the assembled corners onto each side of the G pieces; press seams toward the center.

ASSEMBLING THE QUILT: Refer to the quilt assembly diagram, *opposite below,* as you work.

Sort blocks into six horizontal rows of five blocks each. Sew a 9½-inch-long sashing strip onto the outside (border) edge of the first and last block in each row.

Join rows 2–5 with the shorter sashing units between blocks.

For Row 1, sew a 10½-inch-long red print strip to the tops of the first and last blocks in the row. Press seams toward the red strips. Assemble Row 1 using 10½-inch-long sashing units between the blocks. Press the joining seams toward the sashing.

Start Row 6 by sewing a 10½-inch-long red print strip to the bottoms of the two corner blocks. Assemble Row 6 in the same way as Row 1.

Make four horizontal sashing rows using five sashing units and four setting squares in each row. Each row has a 10½-inch sashing unit at both ends, as shown in the assembly diagram. Press the seams away from setting squares.

Assemble the quilt, alternating block rows with sashing rows.
continued

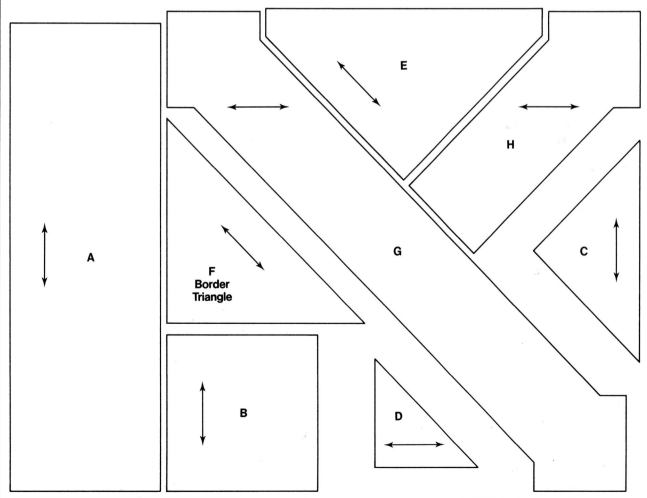

ALBUM BLOCK AND GARDEN MAZE PATTERNS　　　　*Add ¼-inch seam allowances*

A Sampling of Victorian Verse

The Garden Maze quilt pictured on pages 26 and 27 was made in the mid-1800s by friends and relatives of a Harriet Dickerman. The quilt blocks are inscribed in ink with verses, names, and dates ranging from 1850 to 1862. Some also include the name of a town, but only a tantalizing suggestion of the state remains.

We can only speculate about the 12 years between the earliest and latest dates, and about how and why the quilt was made.

Perhaps Harriet collected the blocks from friends over a period of time, finally sewing them together herself before inviting her friends to a quilting bee. It is possible that the blocks were made over a long period of time, and set aside in a hope chest for Harriet's trousseau. Or, perhaps the quilt was made for her as a memorial album of friends and family before she set out to be married somewhere on the frontier. Somehow, it's pleasant to imagine Harriet traveling by covered wagon with this lovely quilt, then brand new, carefully packed away to grace her future home.

The three earliest dated blocks give names and the date of the person's death. Maybe the maker of that block passed away before it could be signed. Or perhaps, some years later, someone else made those blocks in memory of loved ones.

Orando Dickerman and Julia Dickerman both signed blocks in Rockford in April, 1862; three blocks are signed from South Norwalk. The Cornelia Matthews block includes the name of Windham Center, Ma . . . ; the rest of the word disappears into the seam. Maryland? Or Massachusetts? The state of Maine may have a good claim, as the current Post Office directory shows surviving towns of similar names, including one called Windham.

The penned good wishes on these Album blocks are typical of flowery phrases often inscribed on friendship quilts of this period. Although some of the writing is faded past the point of legibility, some of the verses (and the sentiments they express) still are appropriate today.

Here is a sampling of the inscriptions from Harriet's quilt; let them inspire your own verses of friendship.

I the central place will take
surrounded by my friends
Harriet Dickerman

When this you see, remember me
Receive it as a token
Let it remind of actions kind
And words that I have spoken
Grand Mother

With pleasure, dear Harriet,
I make this piece for you.
To put into your bedquilt
If you think it will do.
Susan Warren

I was one of fourteen children
But to me it matters not
If I am by you thus remembered
Peace and love this happy lot
Mary Raymond, April 1854

May you be blessed with all
that Heaven can send
Long life, great pleasures
and many friends
Lucy Johnson

The wintry winds and frost
Can do thee, friend, no harm
For safe within this cabin
thou art snug and warm.
Harriet A. Ward

I know you think me very gay
If colours make me so
But stop my friend and think
How soon I'll fade away
Mary Townsend

For thee a brother fondly prays
May peace and love attend
thy days
And in death's valley dark
and drear,
May Faith and Hope be ever near
Algernon

Thine be every joy and treasure,
Grace, enjoyment, love
and pleasure
And e'er if sorrow prove thy fate,
A faithful friend thou'lt find in
Kate

Dear cousin may sound sleep
to thee Nature's sweet restorer be.
Unsigned

When I am gone and years have
fled, and I lie numbered
with the dead,
May this little token of my love
Send my dear child to God above
Your Mother

In making this, dear cousin,
I have taken pains
And may it oft remind you
Of all our little games
Emeline E. Reed

Harriet,
When this you see
Do remember me
Beda P. Burnham

Our friend who walked by faith
on earth,
And followed God's direction,
Shall be remembered for
her worth
With kind and deep affection.
Aunt Esther

The friends of Harriet Dickerman probably used quill pens to inscribe their good wishes, but today's technology provides other, more lasting, products that are readily available and easy to use.

Craft shops and quilting specialty shops now stock fine point, indelible pens that write in black, blue, red, or brown ink.

Water erasable markers are ideal for writing on fabric names and dates that can be covered with embroidery stitches (see Outline Stitch diagram on page 41).

ZIGZAG BORDER: Join the red and muslin F triangles to make borders. The end border requires two strips—one made up of 23 red and 22 muslin triangles, the other made up of 22 red and 23 muslin triangles. When sewing the two strips together, off-set the triangles to form zigzags. The strips may be uneven at the ends.

Pin end border onto quilt top, matching the centers. Stitch the border in place; trim border strip even with sides of quilt. (Referring to the quilt diagram on page 34, note that partial triangles are cut off at the ends.)

Make the two side border strips the same way. One strip has 28 red and 29 muslin triangles and the other has 29 red and 28 muslin triangles.

Sew side borders onto quilt. Opposite borders are mirror-image.

FINISHING: Cut backing fabric into two 2½-yard lengths. Split one piece lengthwise; sew a narrow panel onto each side of the remaining length.

Layer the backing, batting, and quilt top; baste the three layers together. Quilt as desired. Refer to page 40 for tips on binding.

Album Block Quilt

Shown on page 26.

Finished quilt is approximately 63¾x76½ inches. Each finished block is 9 inches square.

MATERIALS
4⅝ yards of blue print fabric
1¾ yards of white fabric
4½ yards backing fabric
72x90-inch quilt batting
Template material

INSTRUCTIONS
This quilt is made of 30 Album blocks set diagonally with alternating solid squares. The block is exactly the same as the one used in the Garden Maze quilt. Use patterns A, B, C, and D on page 35 for the patchwork block.

CUTTING: From the blue fabric, cut twenty 9½-inch-square solid setting blocks.

For the blue setting triangles, cut five 14-inch squares; cut each of these squares in half diagonally. Then cut nine of the resulting triangles in half diagonally, creating 18 setting triangles that measure 9⅞ inches on the short legs. (The straight of the grain will be on the long edge.)

For the four blue corner triangles, cut two 7¼-inch squares; cut each of these squares in half diagonally to achieve four triangles with the straight of the grain on the shorter legs.

From the remaining blue fabric, cut 120 A rectangles and 240 B squares for the Album blocks. Save the remaining blue fabric for binding.

From the white fabric, cut 30 A rectangles, 60 B squares, 360 C triangles, and 120 D triangles.

ASSEMBLY: Refer to the block instructions on page 34. Make 30 Album blocks.

Join patchwork blocks, plain squares, and all setting triangles into diagonal rows according to the quilt assembly diagram, below. Starting at the upper left corner, assemble rows.

FINISHING: Divide the backing fabric into two 2¼-yard lengths. Split one piece lengthwise and sew a narrow panel onto each side of the wide panel.

Layer the backing, batting, and quilt top; baste the three layers together. Quilt as desired.

See page 40 for tips on binding.

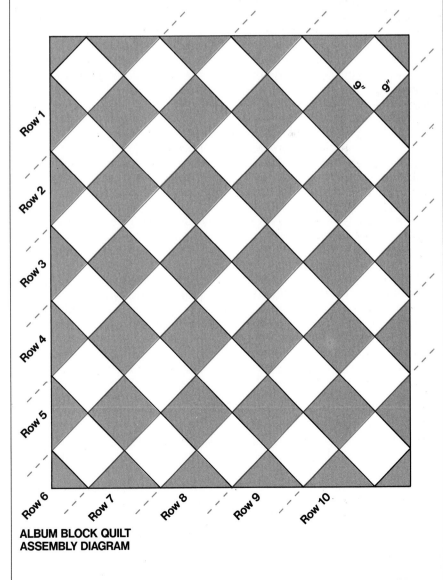

Row 1
Row 2
Row 3
Row 4
Row 5
Row 6
Row 7
Row 8
Row 9
Row 10

9" 9"

**ALBUM BLOCK QUILT
ASSEMBLY DIAGRAM**

Friendship Chain Album Quilt

Shown on page 28.

Finished quilt is approximately 80x93 inches. The finished block is 10 inches square.

MATERIALS
4½ yards of white fabric (includes binding)
2¾ yards of yellow fabric
1 yard *each* of pink and blue fabrics
5½ yards of backing fabric
90x108-inch quilt batting
Template material

INSTRUCTIONS
This quilt is made of 30 pieced blocks set together with sashing between the blocks. Instructions are given for making the scalloped border as shown; it is important to note that the scallops are marked, but not cut until after the quilting is completed so that you can fit the border into a hoop or frame for quilting.

The white A rectangles can be personalized with signatures in permanent marker or embroidery either before or after the blocks are pieced.

CUTTING: Make templates for patterns A, B, C, and the Border Scallop Guide, *opposite*. Patterns A, B, and C are finished size; add ¼-inch seam allowances when cutting these pieces. Do not add seam allowances when using the Border Scallop Guide template.

Measurements given for borders, sashing strips, and sashing squares include ¼-inch seam allowances. Borders are cut longer than needed; trim borders after they are added to the quilt.

From the white fabric, cut two 2½x76-inch border strips, two 2½x90-inch border strips, and seventy-one 3½x10½-inch sashing strips.

From the remaining white fabric, cut 30 A rectangles. There should be approximately ¾ yard of white fabric remaining from

which to cut 20 yards of 1-inch-wide continuous bias for binding (see binding tips on page 40).

From the yellow fabric, cut two 4¼x77-inch border strips, two 4¼x90-inch border strips, and 120 C squares. From the remainder, cut 42 sashing squares, each 3½ inches square.

Cut 180 blue B triangles. From the pink fabric, cut 60 C squares and 60 B triangles.

BLOCK ASSEMBLY: Refer to the block assembly diagram, *right,* as you work.

Sew the long side of a pink triangle to each short side of an A rectangle to form the center unit. Press seams toward triangles.

Join pink and yellow squares and blue triangles in three rows as shown in the upper left section of the diagram. Press so that each row's seams are pressed in different directions. Join the rows to form a large triangle.

In the same manner, make the lower right section of the block. Join large triangles to the sides of the center unit.

Complete 30 pieced blocks.

ASSEMBLY: Join blocks in six horizontal rows with five blocks in each row, placing a muslin sashing strip between blocks and at both ends of each row.

Make seven horizontal sashing rows—use five sashing strips in each row, placing a yellow sashing square between strips and at each end of the rows.

Join block rows and sashing rows, with a row of sashing between each row of blocks. Be sure seam lines of sashing squares align with seams of sashing in the block rows. Finish the assembly with a sashing row at the top and bottom of the quilt. Press seams toward sashing rows.

Sew shorter white borders to top and bottom edges of the quilt top; press seams toward border. Add side borders; miter border corners, trimming excess length.

SCALLOP BORDER: *Note:* Do not cut away the triangles to create the scalloped edges until the quilting is completed.

FRIENDSHIP CHAIN ASSEMBLY DIAGRAM

To mark the yellow border strips, begin by folding each border in half to find the center. Referring to the border diagram, *opposite,* mark triangular scallop outlines, working from the center of each border toward the ends. Shaded areas on the diagram are the areas marked off by the Border Scallop Guide template. Note that the starting positions for the triangular scallops are different for side borders than for the top and bottom borders.

Matching the border centers to the quilt side centers, sew longer borders to the sides of the quilt; trim excess length from border. In the same manner, sew borders to top and bottom of the quilt. Remark corner scallops for correct proportion if needed.

FINISHING: Cut backing fabric into two 2¾-yard lengths. Matching selvage edges and taking ½-inch seams, sew panels together. Trim seam allowances to ¼ inch; press seams to one side.

Layer the quilt back, batting, and quilt top. Baste the three layers together. Quilt as desired.

When the quilting is complete, baste along the marked scallop outlines. Trim away the triangles to create scalloped edges.

Machine-stitch one edge of the bias binding to the right side of the quilt, following the scalloped outline. Turn under ¼ inch on the remaining raw edge of the binding; hand-stitch the folded edge of the binding to the quilt back, clipping points and corners of the scallops as necessary.

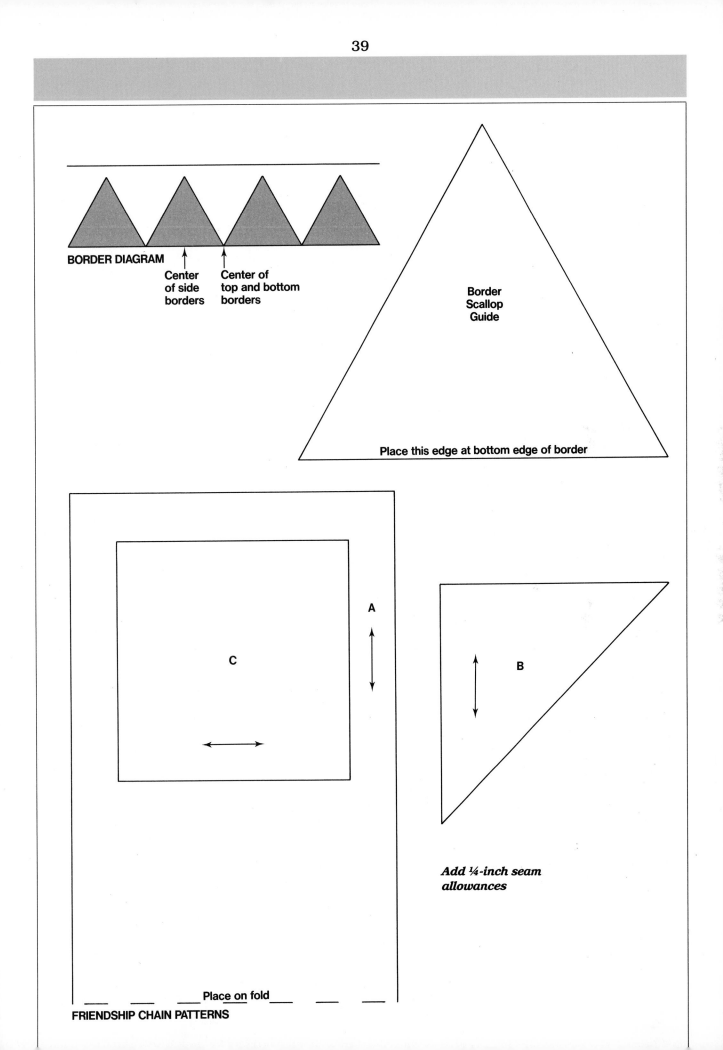

BORDER DIAGRAM

Center of side borders

Center of top and bottom borders

Border Scallop Guide

Place this edge at bottom edge of border

A

C

B

Add ¼-inch seam allowances

Place on fold

FRIENDSHIP CHAIN PATTERNS

Embroidered Signature Quilt

Shown on page 29.

Finished quilt is approximately 69x90 inches. Finished blocks are 15 inches square.

MATERIALS
3¼ yards white or muslin fabric
2⅜ yards pink solid fabric
¾ yard binding fabric
5⅜ yards backing fabric
81x96-inch quilt batting
Pencil or fabric marker
Pink, green, yellow, and black embroidery floss

INSTRUCTIONS
CUTTING: All measurements include ¼-inch seam allowances.

Cut pink fabric into seventeen 2½x85-inch strips. Set aside nine strips for sashing and four strips for side borders. For the checkerboard setting squares, cut 25 inches off each of the remaining four border strips.

Cut a 10-inch-wide panel off one side of the white fabric. From this piece, cut two 2½x80-inch and two 2½x58-inch strips for the border, and five 2½x25-inch strips for the checkerboards.

From remaining white fabric, cut nine 2½x31-inch strips and twelve 15½-inch squares.

BLOCKS: Fold and finger-press to crease vertical and horizontal centerlines in one white square. Match creases with centerlines on embroidery design, *opposite.* Trace design onto fabric square.

Use three strands of embroidery floss to work green vines in outline stitch; the flower centers are done in yellow satin stitch with straight stitches radiating from the center. The pink flower is worked in closely spaced buttonhole stitch.

Trace the name in the center of the block. Stitch the name in black with outline stitches.

Embroider 12 blocks.

SASHING: Cut the nine pink sashing strips into eighteen 2½x31-inch pieces. Seam a pink strip onto each side of a matching white strip. Press seam allowances toward pink fabric.

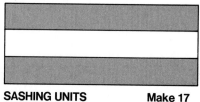

SASHING UNITS   **Make 17 15½" long**

Making and Applying Continuous Binding

Binding is one of the most common methods for finishing the edges of quilts. Straight strips can be used effectively, but bias has a stretch that allows it to curve smoothly around corners; this stretch makes bias desirable for edging quilts with rounded corners and for appliqué projects that require bias-cut strips.

This technique is for French-fold (double thickness) bias binding, which is most durable. If you cut straight-grain strips, follow Step 6 to apply binding.

A 36-inch square of fabric will make enough 2- to 2½-inch-wide binding, bias or straight, to finish most quilts. Always start with a square or rectangle of fabric.

1 Referring to Figure 1, *below,* cut a 36-inch fabric square (or use the full fabric width). Draw a diagonal line from corner to corner. Cut the fabric into two triangles along this line.

2 Using ¼-inch seams, sew the triangles together along the *crosswise* grain as shown in Figure 2, *below.* Press seam open.

3 Use a pencil and ruler to lightly draw horizontal rows across the length of the seamed fabric (Figure 3). The space between rows should equal the desired width of the binding strip, plus seam allowances. Allowing for folding and a ¼-inch seam allowance, a 2- to 2½-inch-wide strip of bias results in a finished binding that is ⅜ inch wide.

4 With right sides together, bring the diagonal ends of the fabric together, but offset the joining by one row or line. Sew the edges together to make a tube (Figure 4); press seams open.

5 Beginning at the top with the first marked line, cut along the pencil line to create a continuous strip of bias binding.

6 With wrong sides together, press the binding strip in half lengthwise. Beginning in the center of any quilt side, sew raw edge of binding to the quilt edge. Corners can be rounded or mitered. Overlap 1 inch of binding at starting point. Trim batting and backing. Turn fold of binding over the raw edge to the back of the quilt; hand-stitch binding to backing.

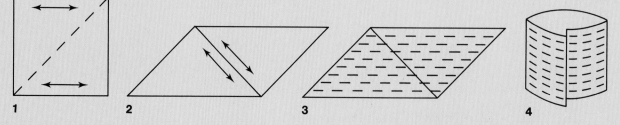

1   2   3   4

Cut each pieced strip in half to obtain 17 sashings, each 15½ inches long. Save the extra sashing in case of error.

SETTING SQUARES: Sew a 25-inch-long pink strip onto both sides of a matching white strip; sew white strips onto both sides of the remaining two pink strips. Press seams toward pink fabric.

Cut each pieced strip into 10 segments, each 2½ inches wide.

Assemble the nine-patch block as illustrated, *below;* press seams toward the center. Make 10 nine-patch checkerboard squares; set four aside for border corners.

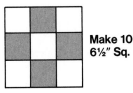

**Make 10
6½" Sq.**

ASSEMBLY: Make two vertical sashing rows by joining three nine-patch squares between four pieced sashing strips. Press seam allowances toward sashings.

Join blocks into three vertical rows of four blocks each, with a pieced sashing sewn between the blocks. Assemble quilt with sashing rows between block rows.

BORDERS: Match white and pink strips of equal length. With each white strip between two pink ones, piece two 6½x80-inch side borders, and two 6½x58-inch end borders.

Compare length of end borders with quilt top; trim excess length. Sew a nine-patch square onto each end of both borders; press seams toward border strips.

Sew side borders onto quilt top; trim edges. Add end borders.

FINISHING: Cut backing fabric into two 96-inch lengths. Sew the two panels together lengthwise.

Layer the backing, batting, and quilt top; baste the three layers together. Quilt as desired.

When quilting is complete, trim batting and backing even with the quilt top.

Cut the binding fabric into 2½-inch-wide bias strips. Sew the strips together, with right sides facing, to make a bias strip that measures approximately 320 inches long. Press the binding in half lengthwise, with the wrong sides together.

Starting at the center of any quilt side, stitch binding to right side of quilt using ¼-inch seams. Overlap the binding edges ½ inch at the starting point. Turn binding over the raw edge; hand-sew to backing.

EMBROIDERED QUILT PATTERN

String Stars Quilt

Shown on pages 30 and 31.

Finished quilt is approximately 84 inches square. The finished blocks are 24 inches square.

MATERIALS

4½ yards of dark green fabric
4½ to 5 yards total of assorted fabric scraps
5 yards of backing fabric
90x106-inch quilt batting
Cardboard or plastic template material
Plastic-coated freezer paper
Rotary cutter and cutting mat
Clear acrylic ruler

INSTRUCTIONS

This string-pieced star is an ideal way for friends to share scraps, or to trade pieced diamonds or stars. Names and dates can be penned or embroidered on the patchwork at random. Completed star blocks are joined in a nine-patch arrangement.

CUTTING: From the green fabric, cut four 6½x88-inch border strips. Measurements for borders include ¼-inch seam allowances. These borders are cut slightly longer than needed; trim them to the correct length when they are added to the quilt top.

Cut nine 11¼-inch squares of green fabric for triangle B. Cut each square into four triangles, cutting each one diagonally from corner to corner both ways. You will have 36 B triangles that include seam allowances.

Cut thirty-six 7½-inch squares from green fabric for square C.

Make a template for Diamond A, expanding the half pattern, *opposite,* into a full diamond. Use the template to cut 72 diamonds from freezer paper. Do not add seam allowances to the paper diamonds. The freezer paper diamonds are used as individual templates to cut the string-pieced fabric diamonds.

STRING-PIECING DIAMONDS: Referring to Photo 1, *below,* use the rotary cutter to cut the patchwork fabrics into 42-inch-long strips. Vary the strip widths from ¾ to 2 inches. Piece short strips together if necessary to achieve the 42-inch length.

Sew together randomly selected strips in a pleasing arrangement of color to assemble a fabric piece 15 to 16 inches wide (Photo 2, *below*). Press seams to one side. Make at least eight different strip sets.

Using a warm dry iron, press the coated side of the paper diamonds onto the wrong side of the pieced fabric as shown in Photo 3, *below.* Space diamonds at least ½ inch apart to allow for seam allowances. Cut out the diamonds, adding ¼-inch fabric seam allowances on all sides. You should be able to cut seven diamonds from each strip set.

Make a variety of diamonds to add interest to your quilt. In addition to string-pieced diamonds, cut some from a single fabric and some that are pieced from two or three large strips of fabric.

Make a total of 72 diamonds.

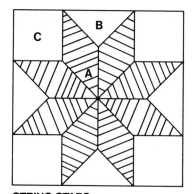

**STRING STARS
ASSEMBLY DIAGRAM**

STAR BLOCKS: Each star is made from eight diamonds. For all steps of the star construction, stitch only on the sewing line (along the edge of the paper, as shown in Photo 4, *opposite*); *do not extend stitching into the seam allowances.* Backstitch at the beginning and end of all seams.

To make a block, use eight diamonds from different strip sets. Join diamonds into four pairs, then sew pairs together to create star halves (Photo 5, *opposite*).

Join the halves, taking care to match all diamond points at the center. Press seam allowances to one side so they fan around the star (Photo 6, *opposite*).

To complete a star block, refer to the assembly diagram, *above.* Set a C square into the corners of the star. Set a B triangle into each of the four remaining openings.

Make nine String Star blocks. Carefully tear the freezer paper off the wrong side of the blocks.

Signatures can be added in ink or with embroidery.

1

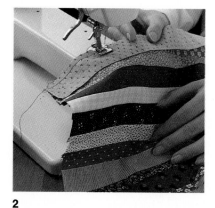

2

3

QUILT ASSEMBLY: Join the blocks into three horizontal rows with three blocks in each row; join the rows.

Sew a border to opposite sides of the quilt; trim excess length. Sew remaining borders to the remaining sides and trim to fit.

FINISHING: Cut backing fabric into two 2½-yard lengths. Split one piece in half lengthwise into two long pieces. Matching selvages and taking ½-inch seams, stitch a half panel onto opposite sides of the full panel; trim seam allowances to ¼ inch.

Layer the backing, batting, and quilt top; baste all layers securely together. Quilt as desired. The quilt shown on pages 30 and 31 is quilted with feathered wreaths in the open areas and repeated semicircles in the borders. The stars are sparsely quilted with straight lines going diagonally across the individual diamonds.

When quilting is complete, trim the batting even with the quilt top. Trim the backing fabric so it is 1 inch larger all around than the quilt top. Fold in the backing ½ inch; bring the folded edge of the quilt back over the edge to the front, creating a self binding. Hand-stitch the folded edge to the front of the quilt.

If you prefer a traditional binding, you will need ¾ yard of fabric to make 340 inches of straight or bias binding. See page 40 for tips on binding.

Add ¼-inch seam allowances

7"

7"

45°

A
½ of Diamond Pattern

Quick cutting instructions are given for triangle B and square C.

Fold

4

5

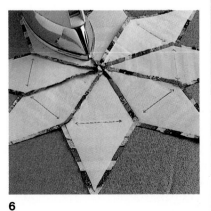

6

HEARTS AND HANDS

FAVORITE SYMBOLS TO MAKE AS GIFTS

A traditional and well-loved token of friendship and affection, the heart-in-hand motif has long been a favorite of quilters and other folk artists. Here is a selection of six gift ideas for you to make, inspired by variations on this familiar theme.

These nearly no-sew projects are fun, contemporary renditions of the popular old Shaker folk design.

A handy bookmark, *below,* is an ideal gift for children to make. Cut shapes from felt, then simply sew or glue the pieces together.

The wall hanging, *right,* is an easy-to-make group gift for kids to create for a teacher, scout leader, or a friend who's moving away.

Fabric "handprints" and inscribed hearts are quickly applied with fusible webbing. An outline of fabric paint provides bold coloration and added dimension.

Patterns and instructions are on page 50.

Two hands, reaching out in friendship, are joined with loving hearts in the machine-appliquéd pillow, *above*.

Also suitable for hand-appliqué if you add seam allowances, the design makes a 10-inch-square pillow that is set off by a luxurious 2½-inch-wide ruffle of coordinating fabric.

As a gesture of affection, this pillow makes a heartwarming gift for any cherished friend, especially if you stitch the design in fabrics to complement the home decor.

Keep a loved one cozy, inside and out, with this handsome wall hanging or lap quilt, *opposite*.

The pattern, Hearts All Around, is pieced and appliquéd to form a 12-inch-square block. Nine blocks are surrounded by a deep, scalloped border in a lush print that gives the 50-inch-square quilt a pleasingly Victorian air.

The matching pillow can be made from the quilt's fabric scraps.

Full-size patterns and instructions for these two projects are on pages 51–55.

Gathered onto a heart-shaped wire form from the local craft shop, this fanciful friendship wreath, *above,* is a country-style frame for the Heart and Hands motif.

A double flounce of fabric is edged with lace and garnished with a bow. Make a simple casing to slide the ruffle easily onto the form.

Use any fabrics you like for this wreath, but for best results, cut the hands and inner ruffle from one small-scale print. Choose a darker, medium-scale floral for the outer ruffle and a monochromatic fabric for the center heart.

Full-size patterns and instructions for this project are on pages 56 and 57.

To complete your cache of gifts, here is an appealing pair of soft-sculpture projects designed especially with collectors in mind.

A sewing friend will love this whimsical heart-in-hands pin cushion, *above right,* fashioned from scraps of fabric and a vintage pair of gloves. Crown your one-of-a-kind creation with an elegant bouquet of ribbon roses.

For button lovers, cover a simple little heart-shaped fabric pin, *above left,* with a multi-tude of antique buttons culled from thrift shops or your own collection.

Full-size patterns and step-by-step instructions for these projects are on pages 54–56.

HEARTS AND HANDS

Heart and Hand Bookmark

Shown on page 44.

The bookmark hand measures 2¾x9½ inches.

MATERIALS
9x12-inch felt square
Scrap felt in contrasting color
Fabric glue
Cardboard or plastic template material
Pinking shears
Pencil or fabric marker

INSTRUCTIONS
Trace hand and heart patterns, *right*, onto template material; cut out the templates.
Trace around the hand template onto the 9x12-inch piece of felt; cut out the hand. Use pinking shears to cut a heart from the contrasting felt. Glue or sew the heart in place on the hand.

Hearts and Hands Wall Hanging

Shown on pages 44 and 45.

Finished wall hanging measures 42 inches square.

MATERIALS
2 yards (54 inches wide) of black wool fabric
7-inch squares of 25 assorted solid or plaid fabrics of silk or cotton for hands; smaller scraps for hearts and border
3 yards of paper-backed fusible webbing
45-inch square of quilt batting
1½ yards backing fabric
Clear or black quilting thread
Four 42-inch-long stretcher bars
Fabric paint in assorted colors
Black permanent pen or marker
Cardboard or plastic template material
Pushpins or thumb tacks
Masking tape
Staple gun

**HEART AND HAND
BOOKMARK PATTERN**

INSTRUCTIONS

This project is ideal for any group since it requires very little sewing. Instructions are given for fusing the hearts and hands, but the piece can be made using traditional appliqué methods if you prefer. The fun part of this project is for everyone involved to use his or her own hand as a pattern.

CUTTING: From the black fabric, cut four border strips, each 5x45 inches. From the remainder, cut a 37-inch square.

Make a template from the heart pattern, *right.* Trace one heart shape for each person, plus 15 to 20 extras, onto the fusible webbing; cut out the hearts.

FUSING: Follow the manufacturer's instructions to apply the hearts of fusible webbing to the wrong sides of the assorted heart fabrics. Fuse the webbing to the wrong sides of the hand fabrics in the same manner.

Once the fabrics are fused to the webbing, each participant can select two favorites—one for the hand, the other for the heart.

The fabrics are much easier to write on when stabilized by the fusible webbing. Each person can sign the right side of the heart fabric with the permanent pen, being careful to confine the writing to within ¼ inch of the edge.

Use a pencil or marker to trace the outline of each person's hand onto the hands fabrics; cut out the hand shapes. Position hands randomly on the large black square, staying at least 1 inch away from each edge. Fuse the hands in place. Fuse a heart on each hand. Fuse extra hearts here and there between the hands.

QUILTING: Quilting is optional, but is recommended for general appearance.

Cut backing fabric 43 inches square. Layer backing and batting under the black square. Baste the three layers together.

By hand or by machine, quilt around some or all of the shapes. Remove the basting thread.

WALL HANGING HEART PATTERN

BORDERS: To make the inner border, use 1½-inch-wide scraps to randomly piece four border strips 38 inches long. Sew borders onto opposite sides, stitching through batting and backing fabric. Sew remaining borders onto remaining sides. Border corners can be square or mitered.

Sewing through all layers, join black borders to the center block; miter corners.

FINISHING: Assemble the four stretcher bars.

Center the fabric piece on the stretcher bars. Keeping the top fabric out of the way, stretch the backing fabric taut on the frame; tape the backing fabric in place.

Pull one black border taut over the stretcher bar; tack it in place. Repeat for the opposite border, then the remaining two borders. Adjust borders until the fabric is stretched taut and square over the stretcher bars.

Begin stapling in the center of each strip, working toward the corners. Stop stapling about 1 inch from each corner.

Match the mitered seam of the border with the mitered joining of the frame. Put one staple in the center on the back side, straddling the seam.

Make a small pleat by rolling in the excess fabric on either side of the corner; staple the pleat to the frame. Finish all four corners.

Following the manufacturer's directions, use fabric paints to cover the exposed raw edges of the hearts and hands. Let the paints dry before hanging.

Hearts All Around Wall Hanging

Shown on page 47.

Wall hanging is approximately 50 inches square. Finished size of each block is 12 inches square. The pillow is 14¼ inches square excluding a 2½-inch-wide ruffle.

MATERIALS

2 yards of white and blue print background fabric
½ yard *each* of pink print and blue dot fabrics
2⅛ yards of blue floral fabric for block squares, borders, quilt binding, and pillow ruffle
¼ yard of pink checked fabric for pillow ruffle
3 yards of backing fabric
58-inch square of quilt batting
Plastic template material
Polyester stuffing for pillow
Nonpermanent fabric marker

INSTRUCTIONS

This wall quilt is made of nine blocks set together in three rows. The 7-inch-wide floral border is finished with scalloped corners.

The matching one-block pillow can be made from remnants of the quilt fabrics.

Making the quilt

CUTTING: From the floral border fabric, cut borders on the lengthwise grain. Cut two border strips 8x38 inches and two strips 8x53 inches. (These borders are cut slightly longer than needed; they are cut to match the length of the quilt after they are sewn to the quilt edge.)

Cut a 22-inch square of floral fabric for the quilt binding and a 16x42-inch strip for the pillow borders and ruffle.

Make templates for patterns A through F on page 52. These full-size patterns do not include seam allowances; add a ¼-inch seam allowance to each pattern piece when cutting. Mark the top and center seam edges of templates A, B, and C, as shown on patterns. Mark grain lines on all templates.
continued

From remaining blue floral fabric, cut 36 *each* of pieces E and F.

From print background fabric, cut 36 *each* of pieces A and C. Flip the template over to cut 36 *each* of A and C reversed.

Cut 36 *each* of B and B reversed from the blue dot fabric. Cut 36 *each* of D and D reversed from the pink print fabric.

Save the scraps of each fabric to cut pieces for the pillow.

BLOCK ASSEMBLY: One block is made of four 6-inch squares. Each quarter-block has a left side (pieces A, B, C, and D reversed) and a right side (A reversed, B reversed, C reversed, and D).

Assemble pieces A, B, and C as shown in the assembly diagram, *right*. Join reversed pieces in the same way to make the right side of the quarter-block.

It is advisable to sew all the left sides first, then all right sides, to avoid getting the pieces mixed up. Make 36 of each side.

Using the pattern layout, *below,* trace and cut an appliqué placement guide from template plastic. Trace the left half of the square as drawn, including the half-heart outline; add a ¼-inch seam allowance on the outside edges. Cut away the heart outline.

Position the placement guide atop each unit, flipping the plastic as necessary to align outside edges of the template and the pieced unit. Mark the half-heart

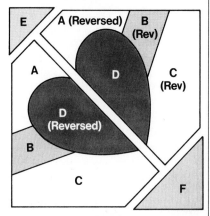

**HEARTS ALL AROUND
¼-BLOCK ASSEMBLY DIAGRAM**

outline lightly with nonpermanent fabric marker.

Turn the *curved* edge of the half-heart (D) under ¼ inch; clip the seam allowance as necessary. Matching the *straight* edge of the D piece with the center seam edge of the ABC unit, position the half-heart on the drawn outline.

Appliqué curved heart edge in place; press. Trim pieced fabric from under the heart, leaving a ¼-inch seam allowance.

With right sides together, stitch the center seam joining right and left units. Press seam allowance to one side. Complete the quarter-block by adding E and F triangles. Make 36 quarter-blocks.

Sew four of the quarter-blocks together to complete one block. The larger triangles (F) are always positioned in the outside corners. Make nine blocks.

QUILT ASSEMBLY: Sew blocks together into three rows of three

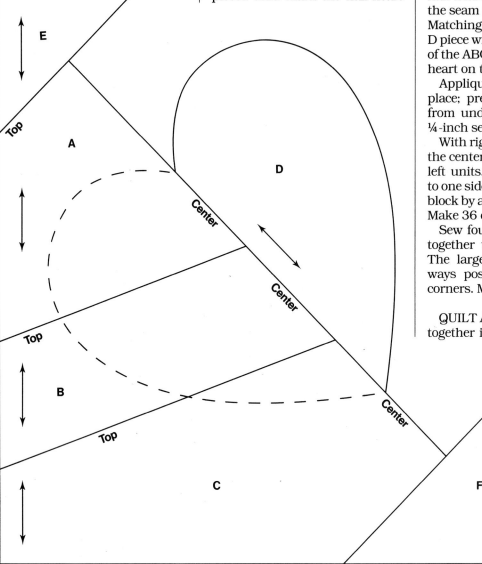

HEARTS ALL AROUND PATTERNS

Add ¼-inch seam allowances

blocks each. Join rows to complete center section of the quilt.

Sew short borders to opposite sides of the quilt top; trim excess length. Press seams toward borders. Sew longer borders to remaining sides.

Make a paper or plastic template of the corner scallop pattern, *right.* Trace the pattern onto the fabric on both sides of each corner, flipping it at the indicated center line to fit it to the adjacent side. Cut at least one scallop at each corner, leaving the border between corners straight. Adding additional scallops is optional.

FINISHING: Cut backing fabric into two 1½-yard lengths. Cut one piece in half lengthwise. Sew one narrow panel onto each side of the full panel; trim backing to approximately 58 inches square.

Layer the backing, batting, and quilt top; baste all three layers securely together. Quilt as desired, then remove basting except at corners. Trim batting and backing fabric even with quilt top.

Use the 22-inch square of floral fabric to make at least 210 inches of continuous bias binding (see tips on page 40).

Sew binding to quilt edge, beginning at the middle of any side. As you approach the scallop, leave the needle down (in the fabric) while you pin the binding around the curve (see illustration, *below*). Ease the fullness of the binding so it matches the curve.

Do not backstitch at the inside corner. Leave the needle down; lift the presser foot and pivot the quilt to align the needle with the next side of the curve. With the needle still in the quilt, pin the binding around the new curve and continue to sew (see illustration, *below*). Use a long straight pin or the point of a seam ripper to help you maneuver the fabric under the presser foot.

Turn binding over to the quilt back. Hand-sew binding to backing, mitering corners.

Making the pillow

CUTTING: Cut the 16x42-inch blue floral fabric into three ruffle strips 4x42 inches and four border strips 2x18 inches. Cut the pink check ruffle fabric into three strips 2½x42 inches.

From remnants of the quilt materials, cut 15½-inch squares of backing, batting, and fabric for the pillow back, as well as pieces to make one block.

ASSEMBLY: Make one Hearts All Around block as described. Sew two floral borders to opposite sides of the completed block; trim excess length. Sew the remaining borders to opposite sides. Press seam allowances toward borders.

Layer backing, batting, and pillow top; baste. Quilt as desired. Trim excess batting and backing even with pillow top.

Seam pink ruffle strips end to end; press seam allowances open. Repeat for blue ruffle strips. Sew the pink and blue strips together along one long edge; press seam toward darker fabric.

Bring ends of the long strip together and stitch, making a continuous circle of the pieced ruffle fabric. Press this seam open.

Press the ruffle fabric in half, matching raw edges, with right sides out. Run two lines of machine basting close to the raw edges of the strip. Gather ruffle to fit pillow top. Baste ruffle around the edge of the pillow top, matching right sides.

Lay pillow back over pillow top with right sides together. Stitch ½ inch from the edge around the pillow. Leave a 6-inch opening in the middle of one side for turning. Turn right side out. Stuff pillow; slip-stitch opening closed.

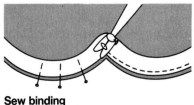

Sew binding
to scalloped edge

**HEARTS ALL AROUND
CORNER SCALLOP GUIDE**

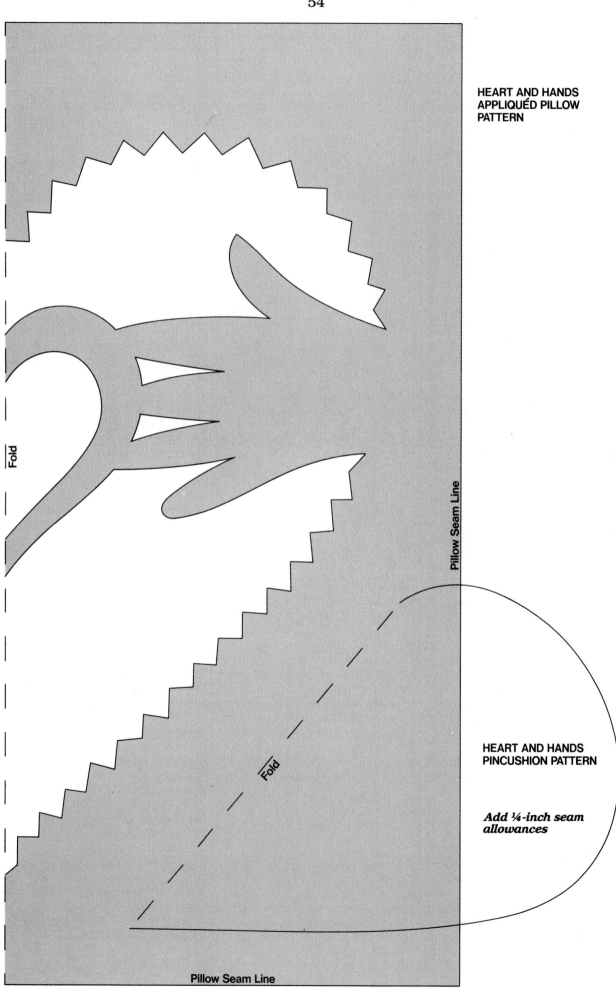

HEART AND HANDS
APPLIQUÉD PILLOW
PATTERN

Fold

Pillow Seam Line

Fold

HEART AND HANDS
PINCUSHION PATTERN

*Add ¼-inch seam
allowances*

Pillow Seam Line

Heart and Hands Appliquéd Pillow

Shown on page 46.

The pillow is 10 inches square excluding a 2½-inch-wide ruffle.

MATERIALS
¾ yard of print fabric for front, back, and ruffle
11-inch square of blue fabric
⅛ yard of solid fabric for center heart and piping
1½ yards of narrow piping cording
10-inch square pillow form
⅓ yard paper-backed fusible webbing

INSTRUCTIONS
These instructions are written for machine-appliqué, but the pillow can be made using traditional appliqué methods, if you prefer. For machine-appliqué, it is not necessary to add seam allowances to the pattern.

CUTTING: From the print fabric, cut two 6x42-inch strips for the ruffle. From the remainder, cut two 11-inch squares. Set one square aside for the back.

FUSING: Trace the pattern, *opposite,* onto the paper side of the fusible webbing. Following manufacturer's instructions, fuse webbing with the traced design onto the wrong side of the blue appliqué fabric.
Following the traced line on the paper, cut out the center design. Leave the outside edges of the square intact. Peel the paper backing off the webbing; position the blue fabric atop the print square, matching outside edges. Fuse the blue fabric in place.
In the same manner, trace the center heart onto a 3-inch square of fusible webbing; fuse a pink heart in place on the design.

APPLIQUÉ: Set the sewing machine to make a narrow, closely spaced zigzag stitch. If you are not experienced in machine-ap-

pliqué, practice on scraps before stitching on your pillow design. Practice stitching curves and points for the center heart and pivoting at corners for the jagged edges of the large heart outline.
Using pink thread, machine-appliqué around the center heart, sewing through all layers. Use blue thread to appliqué the rest of the design.

FINISHING: Make 43 inches of 1-inch-wide continuous bias for the pink piping (see tips on bias on page 40). Use a zipper foot to sew the fabric over the cording. Trim the exposed seam allowances to ½ inch. Matching raw edges of piping and pillow top, baste piping around the outside edge of the pillow top.
Taking a ¼-inch seam allowance, seam the ruffle strips together to make an 83½-inch-long strip. Seam the ends of the strip together to make a circle. Press seam allowances open.
Fold the ruffle strip in half, right side out. Press the 3-inch-wide strip, raw edges together.
Run two lines of machine basting close to the raw edges of the ruffle strip. Gather the ruffle to fit around the pillow top; pin the ruffle in place, matching raw edges. Do not skimp on ruffle fabric around the corners as this will make the ruffle curl inward when finished. Baste the ruffle onto the pillow top over the piping.
With right sides facing, sew the back onto the pillow top on the ½-inch seam line; leave a 7-inch opening in the middle of one side for turning and stuffing.
Trim seam allowance and clip corners; turn the pillow right side out. Be sure to push the corners out completely. Insert the pillow form; slip-stitch the seam opening closed.

Heart and Hands Pincushion

Shown on page 49.

The heart pincushion measures 7 inches across.

MATERIALS
One pair of gloves
¼ yard of vertical striped fabric
24 inches of ⅜-inch-wide burgundy picot-edged ribbon
20 inches *each* of ⅛-inch-wide antique gold twist, black satin twist, ½-inch-wide gold ribbon, and ¾-inch-wide burgundy grosgrain ribbon
28 inches *each* of ⅜-inch-wide black satin ribbon and 1-inch-wide black pregathered lace
Polyester filling
6-inch square of cardboard
White crafts glue; toothpicks
Antique gold spray paint
One ⅜-inch-round gold shank button
Tracing paper and pencil

INSTRUCTIONS
HEART: Trace the half-heart pattern, *opposite.* Use the paper pattern to cut two complete hearts from the striped fabric, adding ¼-inch seam allowances. Position the fabric so the stripes run vertically through the heart.
From the remaining stripe fabric, cut two 1½x11-inch strips for the boxing welt. Sew these two strips together, end to end, to make one 20½-inch long strip. Press the seam open.
Match the center seam of the pieced welt strip with the top center of the front heart fabric, right sides together. Pin the strip around the heart, letting both ends hang past the bottom of the heart. The strip is longer than needed, but do not trim excess.
Starting at the bottom point, stitch strip to heart. Press seam; then sew the ends of the strip together, with the seam directly at the tip of the heart. Trim seam allowance to ¼ inch.
Sew back heart to raw edge of the center strip, beginning at the
continued

bottom point. Leave 2 to 3 inches open for turning. Turn the heart right side out; stuff firmly. Stitch the opening closed by hand.

"Antique" the black lace by spraying it very lightly with gold paint; let paint dry completely.

Beginning at the bottom of the heart, hand-sew the lace around the heart, about ¼ inch behind the front seam.

Couch burgundy picot-edged ribbon over the bottom edge of the black lace, so the picots cover the seam. Overlap ribbon ends at bottom point.

RIBBON ROSES: Narrow strips of ribbons make small roses; wider strips make larger roses. The centers can be adjusted to recede into the flower or they can be pushed out to prominence.

Horizontally lay a 14-inch piece of black satin ribbon wrong side down on a flat surface. Bring 3 inches of the left side down over the ribbon at a right angle. Lay a toothpick on the extreme left side of the 3-inch vertical section and roll the ribbon around it until you reach the opposite edge. Remove the toothpick and grasp ribbon tube at the bottom.

Fold the top of the ribbon away from you at about a 30-degree angle. Continuing to roll to the right, roll ribbon around until you run out of tube. Fold the ribbon away from you again at a 30-degree angle, and roll it up again. Repeat until rose is the desired size. Adjust the center up and down to achieve the look you like.

Pin and sew all the edges together at the bottom of the rose. Leave 2- to 3-inch tails at the beginning and end of each rose. Use ribbons to make two black roses, one gold, and one burgundy.

Run a gathering stitch along one edge of a 5-inch piece of the burgundy grosgrain; gather ribbon to make a small flower. Sew the gold button in the center of the gathered flower.

Cut the black satin twist in half. To prevent fraying, lightly apply glue to cut ends with a toothpick. Tie into two bows.

Arrange the roses and bows as desired, tacking them in place on the front heart.

Make a bow in the middle of the gold twist. Sew the bow in place, then couch the meandering tails over the heart.

FINISHING: Use a pencil or crochet hook to push stuffing into the fingertips of the gloves. Stuff gloves firmly.

Cut two oval shapes from the cardboard to fit securely into the wrist opening of the gloves. Cover the cardboard with fabric, gluing excess fabric to the back of the cardboard. Slip ovals into gloves to keep the fiberfill from coming out. Glue in place.

Tack the heart to the palms of the gloves.

Button Heart Pin

Shown on page 49.

The heart pin measures approximately 3 inches tall.

MATERIALS
4-inch square of tan fabric
3-inch square of cardboard
Two 3-inch squares of low-loft quilt batting
3-inch square of ultrasuede or felt for backing
1-inch metal pin back
Hot glue gun or thick white crafts glue
6 inches of ⅛-inch-wide gold ribbon
Three-faceted black jet beads
Three ⅜-inch pearl buttons
13 gold metal buttons, ranging in size and shape from ½-inch diameter to 1¼-inch diameter
Tracing paper and pencil

INSTRUCTIONS
Trace heart pattern, *opposite, left,* then glue tracing onto the cardboard square; cut out heart shape. Use cardboard to trace heart on batting, backing, and fabric squares, drawing lightly on the right side of the fabrics. Cut out batting and backing hearts.

Sew buttons onto fabric square within the heart outline. Start with the largest, working to the smallest. Overlap buttons as you place and sew them. The pin will be seen from above, so look at it from this angle when deciding the placement of the buttons.

Sew a bow of gold ribbon in place on one side.

Place the layers of batting on the cardboard heart and the fabric with buttons atop the batting. Clip the edges of the fabric square to within ⅛ inch of the cardboard.

Pull the excess fabric from the front to the back; secure edges with glue. While the glue is wet, smooth the heart edges by overlapping the clipped fabric.

Sew the metal pin to the backing, ½ inch down from the top.

When dry, place the backing on the back of the button/heart assembly, covering the folds of excess fabric. Glue to secure.

Heart and Hands Fabric Wreath

Shown on page 48.

The wreath measures 10 inches across excluding a 2½-inch-wide ruffle.

MATERIALS
10-inch diameter heart-shaped wire wreath form (available at crafts supply stores)
⅜ yard *each* of pink print and taupe floral fabrics
5x10-inch scrap of blue fabric
2⅓ yards of ¼-inch-wide lace
2 yards of ⅝-inch-wide beige grosgrain ribbon
5 inches of florist's wire
Polyester filling

INSTRUCTIONS
The wreath is a double-layered ruffle threaded onto a wire form. Most commercially available wire forms open at the bottom of the heart and come with a ring or a plastic tip to close the ends. The hands are tacked in place on the back of the ruffle.

RUFFLE: Cut two 6½x43-inch strips of taupe fabric. Sew strips together to make one strip 84 inches long; press seam open.

Baste lace to one long edge on the right side of the strip, matching raw edges. Fold fabric strip in half lengthwise, wrong sides together and matching raw edges. Stitch a ¼-inch seam along the long edge of the strip; turn tube right side out through an open end. Press tube with lace extending from the top seamed edge.

Cut two 4x42-inch strips of pink fabric and make a tube in the same manner, omitting the lace. Press the pink tube with the long seam in the middle of the back side so it will be hidden from view on the finished wreath.

Pin pink strip atop the wider taupe strip, with bottom edge of pink strip ⅜ inch from bottom of the taupe strip. Sew the strips together by top stitching ⅛ inch from the edge of the pink strip. Top stitch a second line ¼ inch from the first stitching line.

Thread ruffle onto wire form through the channel; adjust gathers evenly. Bring the ruffle ends together at the bottom of the heart, right sides together. Sew a seam by hand or machine from the edge right up to the channel. Replace closing tips on wire ends.

HEART AND HANDS: Cut two 5-inch squares of the blue fabric. Trace the heart pattern, *below right,* onto the wrong side of one square and cut a small slit in the center of the drawn heart. Sew on the drawn line around the entire shape, using a very small stitch length. Trim the seam allowance to ¼ inch; clip to stitching line at the top center point of the heart.

Turn heart right side out; stuff. The back of the heart will not be visible, so you can use large overcast stitches to close the slit.

From the remaining pink fabric, cut four 6-inch lengths. Trace the hand pattern onto the wrong sides of two pieces. Match each marked fabric with a plain piece. Stitch on marked lines; leave openings as indicated on pattern. Trim seam allowance to ¼ inch; clip to stitching lines between fingers and at wrists.

Turn hands right side out; use a long, thin object to push stuffing into finger tips. Stuff hands; hand-sew openings closed.

Position the hands and heart as shown in the photo on page 48, underlapping the tiny inner ruffle of the wreath. Tack the fingertips under the center heart on both sides; tack the wrist ends of the hands under the ruffle.

Use 42 inches of grosgrain ribbon to make a bow. Secure bow loops with florist's wire. Cut remaining ribbon in half; wire both pieces to back of bow, centering each piece. Curl ribbon tails by drawing them against a scissor blade. Tack bow at top of wreath.

Use a 5-inch length of ribbon to make a hanging loop; tack the loop to the back of the wreath just below the top of the upper ruffle.

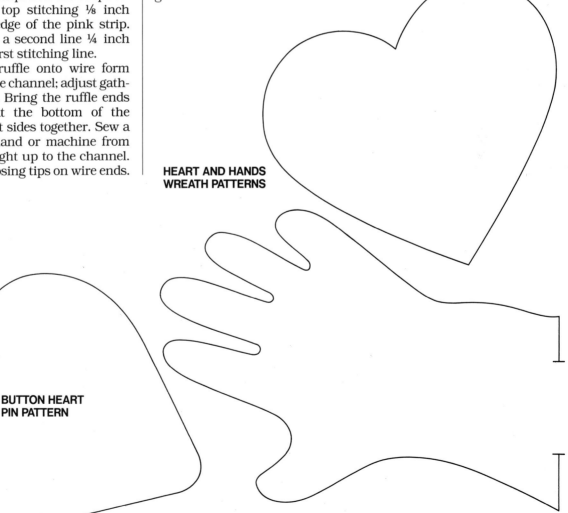

HEART AND HANDS WREATH PATTERNS

BUTTON HEART PIN PATTERN

CELEBRATING FRIENDSHIP

SPECIAL OCCASIONS

Weddings and births, holidays and homecomings, commencements, birthdays, retirements, and family reunions—these are some of the special events that might be commemorated with a friendship quilt. Your love and pride will be appreciated and remembered many years from now if they are expressed in a lasting gift from your own hands. This chapter offers a sampling of projects to inspire your gesture of respect and affection.

The striking "Friends Among the Pines" quilt, *right,* is the work of a Minnesota quilters' group in honor of their outgoing president.

True to tradition, Marilyn Ginsburg designed the 8-inch-square block herself—a personal interpretation of a favorite old pine tree motif worked in her favorite colors of brown and green.

Thirty members of "Quilters Along the Yellowstone Trail"

tackled a pile of scraps. The result is 30 tree blocks, each pieced with muslin and a random assortment of forest green-colored fabrics.

Set on the diagonal with alternating four-patch squares, each tree block is inscribed in brown permanent ink with the name and town of the maker. The finished quilt is 72¼x87½ inches.

For step-by-step instructions for this quilt, turn to page 64.

CELEBRATING FRIENDSHIP

Appliquéd by hand and lavished with ribbon and lace, this richly romantic wall quilt, *opposite,* is an elegant gift for a bride from her closest friends.

Each of the six charming designs fits in a 7¾-inch square. Use the motifs individually for smaller bridal shower gifts, too, such as a ring pillow or an album cover.

Full-size patterns and instructions for this quilt begin on page 66.

To turn a slumber party into a memorable occasion, make this ready-to-autograph sleeping bag and pillowcase, *above.*

Amid giggles and jokes, your child can collect on-the-spot mementos—the muslin lining provides the perfect canvas for handwritten notes. Tuck in a supply of colored permanent markers to take along.

Complete instructions begin on page 72.

CELEBRATING FRIENDSHIP

Be a booster and stitch up a jazzy felt stadium blanket, *opposite,* to commemorate a championship season or to showcase collectibles.

For a player or a loyal fan, include everything from autographs and a pair of lucky socks to pins, pennants, and varsity letters. Long after graduation, the blanket will remind an armchair quarterback of his glory days.

Celebrate the feats of any teen with a quilt of scout patches or prize ribbons, for example.

Winsome animals with heart-shaped balloons, *above,* make this a cheerful crib quilt for a new baby. Made by hand or entirely by machine, this is an ideal project for a small group to stitch up for a baby shower.

If more friends want to join the party, suggest they use matching fabrics to create coordinating accessories such as crib bumpers or a diaper bag.

Full-size patterns and instructions for both quilts begin on page 74.

"Friends Among the Pines" Quilt

Shown on pages 58 and 59.

Finished quilt measures approximately 72¼x87½ inches. Each finished block is 8 inches square.

MATERIALS
1⅝ yards of muslin
Assorted "tree" fabrics (red, brown, blue, green, and tan prints) in 1½-inch-wide strips totaling 1 yard
Fifteen 5-inch squares of assorted green print fabrics for tree top bases
Fifteen 3x5-inch pieces of assorted brown prints for the tree trunks
Eighty 4½-inch squares of assorted dark prints for the four-patch blocks
1¼ yards of brown print for setting triangles
2⅛ yards of brown plaid fabric for the outside border
⅔ yard of green print for the inside border
¾ yard of binding fabric
5¼ yards of backing fabric
81x96-inch quilt batting
Rotary cutter, cutting board, and acrylic ruler

INSTRUCTIONS
For some members of "Quilters Along the Yellowstone Trail," the pine tree blocks were a learning experience in accuracy. The small squares in the piecing require careful cutting and stitching.

Marilyn Ginsburg selected and precut all the fabrics for her quilt, and each quilter chose her favorites from which to make a block. The name and town of the maker is penned with an indelible marker at the base of each tree.

A ¼-inch seam allowance is used throughout these instructions. All measurements given for cutting include seam allowances. No patterns are necessary for this block, as it is easy to measure and cut all the pieces with a ruler and rotary cutter.

CUTTING: *Note:* The number of pieces to cut for a single block is

listed first; the number of pieces needed to make the entire quilt is shown in parentheses.

From the brown print(s), cut one (30) 1½x5-inch tree trunk.

Cut one (15) 4⅞-inch square(s) from green print fabric(s) for the tree base(s). Cut the square(s) in half *diagonally* to obtain triangular bases for two (30) tree blocks.

Cut the assorted "tree" fabrics into 1½-inch squares. Select 19 (570) squares of different fabrics for each block.

From the muslin, cut one (30) 1½x30-inch strip(s) for the tree block(s). Cut the strip(s) into 20 (600) 1½-inch squares. From the remaining muslin fabric, cut one (15) 6½-inch square(s). Cut the square in quarters *diagonally* to obtain four (60) background triangles, enough for two blocks.

For the brown print setting triangles, cut five 13½-inch squares and two 8-inch squares. Cut both 8-inch squares in half diagonally to obtain four corner triangles. Cut each of the large squares into *quarters* diagonally to obtain 18 triangles (plus two extra triangles). *Note:* The setting triangles are slightly larger than necessary; the extra is cut away when the border is added.

The green inside border strips are cut on the crosswise grain and pieced to fit the assembled quilt top. Cut eight 2½x42-inch green print strips for the border.

Cut four 8½-inch-wide strips down the length of the brown plaid fabric for the outer border. These strips are longer than necessary, but will be cut to fit after they are sewn onto the quilt top.

PINE TREE BLOCK: From the 1½-inch squares, use 20 muslin and 19 print fabric squares to make one pine tree block.

Selecting print fabrics randomly, assemble seven (210) of Unit A and six (180) of Unit B as shown in Figure 1, *below.* Each sewn unit measures 1½x3½ inches. Press seams toward print fabrics.

Alternating A and B units, sew these three-square pieces together to form one (30) of Unit X and one (30) of Unit Y as illustrated in Figure 2, *below.* Adjust the seam allowances as necessary to obtain the correct finished size. Press all the joining seam allowances in the same direction.

Sew Unit X to one side of the tree base triangle, then add Unit Y as shown in Figure 3, *opposite.* Press seams toward triangle.

Note that one muslin square on both units extends past the base triangle. Mark an extension of the triangle base across the muslin squares as shown in Figure 3; use this as a placement line when adding the trunk unit, then trim the excess muslin.

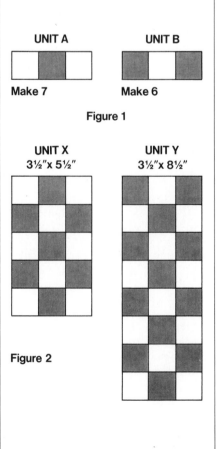

UNIT A   UNIT B

Make 7   Make 6

Figure 1

UNIT X
3½"x 5½"

UNIT Y
3½"x 8½"

Figure 2

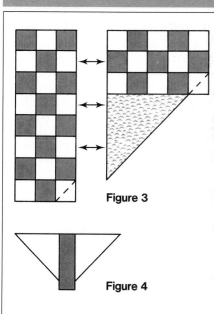

Figure 3

Figure 4

Sew a muslin background triangle to either side of the trunk piece as shown in Figure 4, *above;* be careful not to stretch the bias edges of the triangles. Press seams toward trunk.

Join the tree top to the trunk section, matching centers. Press seam toward the tree top.

Using a ruler and rotary cutter, square up the completed block by cutting the excess trunk fabric even with the edge of the 8½-inch block. Make 30 pine tree blocks.

FOUR-PATCH BLOCKS: Selecting fabrics randomly, join four 4½-inch squares of print fabric to make one 8½-inch block. Make 20 four-patch blocks.

QUILT ASSEMBLY: Lay out all the completed tree blocks, the four-patch blocks, and the setting triangles following the quilt assembly diagram, *right.*

Join the blocks and triangles in 10 diagonal rows (indicated by red lines on the diagram); press joining seams of alternating rows in opposite directions.

Join rows; press all seams from joining rows in the same direction. Add corner triangles.

Using the ruler and rotary cutter, trim excess fabric from side

triangles. Make certain to leave seam allowances beyond the corners of the blocks. Opposite sides of the quilt should measure the same and the corners should be at right angles.

BORDERS: Measure the sides of the quilt. Piece 2½-inch-wide green print strips as necessary to obtain the length needed for two side borders. Sew borders to quilt sides; press seams toward borders. Repeat for the top and bottom green borders.

Sew a brown outside border strip to each quilt side; trim excess length. Repeat for the top and bottom borders. Press seams toward inside borders.

FINISHING: Cut backing fabric into two 2⅜-yard lengths. Seam the two pieces together; press the seam allowance to one side.

Layer the quilt backing, batting, and pieced top. Baste the three layers together securely.

Quilt as desired. The quilt pictured on pages 58 and 59 has simple outline quilting around the outside edge of each tree top and on the background triangles to outline the trunks. Do outline quilting or choose suitable quilting motifs for the four-patch blocks and the borders.

Cut 2¼-inch-wide strips of the binding fabric on the bias or straight grain. Refer to page 40 for tips on applying binding.

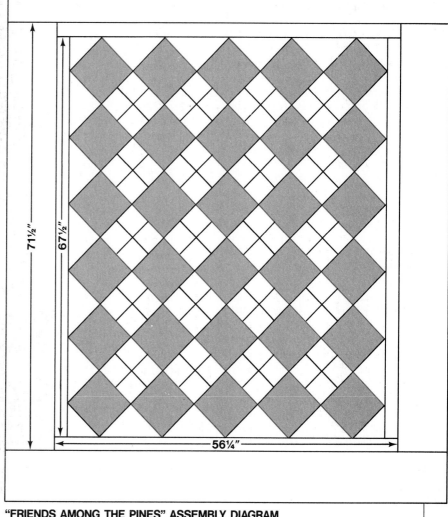

71½"

67½"

56¼"

"FRIENDS AMONG THE PINES" ASSEMBLY DIAGRAM

Bridal Shower Wall Hanging

Pictured on page 60.

The finished wall hanging is 41 inches square. Each of the appliqué blocks is 7¾ inches square.

MATERIALS:

1¼ yards of peach fabric
¾ yard of cream fabric
¼ yard of blue fabric
⅛ yard, or scraps, *each* of
  yellow, green, brown, white,
  and pink fabrics
1¼ yards of backing fabric
1½ yards of quilt batting
1⅜ yards of 1-inch-wide cream
  satin ribbon for bells
¾ yard of ¼-inch-wide blue
  satin ribbon for bouquet
¼ yard *each* of ⅛-inch-wide
  satin ribbon in pink, blue,
  and cream for "shower" gifts
1 yard of 2-inch-wide flat lace
  for bouquet
12 inches of ½-inch-wide flat
  lace for cake
Embroidery floss in yellow,
  pink, and brown
11 to 26 purchased ribbon roses
  for wedding cake
Blue permanent pen or marker
  for envelope
Silver metallic thread for parasol
  quilting
Nonpermanent fabric marker
Template material

INSTRUCTIONS

This appliqué can be done by machine, but only by those with advanced skills. Instructions are given for hand appliqué.

There are several methods of transferring appliqué patterns and placement lines onto fabric. If you prefer a method other than the one described here, adapt the instructions accordingly.

CUTTING: Measurements given for cutting instructions include ¼-inch seam allowances.

From the cream fabric, cut two 12¼-inch squares. Cut both squares in quarters *diagonally* to obtain eight setting triangles.

For corner triangles, cut two 6½-inch squares of cream fabric.

Cut both squares in half *diagonally* to obtain four triangles.

Cut four 8¼-inch squares from the remaining cream fabric for the setting blocks.

From the peach fabric, cut four 5½x42½-inch border strips, then cut nine 8¼-inch squares.

APPLIQUÉ: Templates for hand appliqué usually are made without seam allowances. Using the patterns *below* and on pages 67–71, trace the black outline of each shape directly onto the template plastic. Blue lines indicate

embellishments such as embroidery or ribbon. Make a template for each appliqué shape.

Place a template faceup on the right side of the appropriate appliqué fabric. Draw around the template *lightly*, using a pencil or nonpermanent marker. This line is the *sewing* line of the piece. Cut the appliqué shape from the fabric, adding a seam allowance of approximately ¼ inch.

Cut four of the wedding bells pattern, *opposite*, from blue fabric; cut clappers from yellow fabric. The church and steeple, the

**BRIDAL SHOWER
WALL HANGING
PATTERN**

four-layer cake, the shower parasol, and the invitation envelope all are cut from white fabric.

Use scraps of other fabrics to cut the small appliqué pieces.

To mark placement guides on the background fabric, center an 8½-inch square of peach fabric over each pattern. Lightly trace the outline of the design on the right side of the fabric.

Turn under seam allowances, then baste pieces in place. Do not turn under edges that will be covered by another appliqué (such as the top of a tree trunk where it is covered by the tree top).

Clip into the seam allowance where it is necessary to smooth a curve, such as in the bouquet of flowers or the tree tops.

Pin or baste the appliqué pieces for each pattern onto the background square so that the placement lines are covered.

Appliqué with a blind stitch, using a thread color that matches the appliqué fabric. When appliqué is complete, trim away the background fabric from behind the design to reduce bulk.

BOUQUET: Gather the 2-inch-wide lace to fit the inner circle of the bouquet as shown, *opposite*. Hand-sew the bottom edge of the lace onto the background square.

Appliqué randomly positioned leaves and multi-colored flowers in the center of the circle, positioning flowers to cover the bottom edge of the lace. Use yellow

floss to make a cluster of French knots in the center of each flower.

Cut the blue ribbon in half; make a bow with the two pieces. Tack the bow in place on the bouquet; tie knots in the ribbon tails.

BELLS: Positioning the clapper under the bell, sew the left bell in place first. Next, stitch the bottom (inside) of the right bell; leave the top edge flat where it is overlapped by the main bell piece. Sew the clapper in place, then stitch the bell over the flat edge.

Make four wedding bell blocks.

Cut the 1-inch-wide ribbon into four equal lengths. Make a bow for each block; tack a bow at the top of the bells as shown, *below*.
continued

**BRIDAL SHOWER
WALL HANGING
PATTERN**

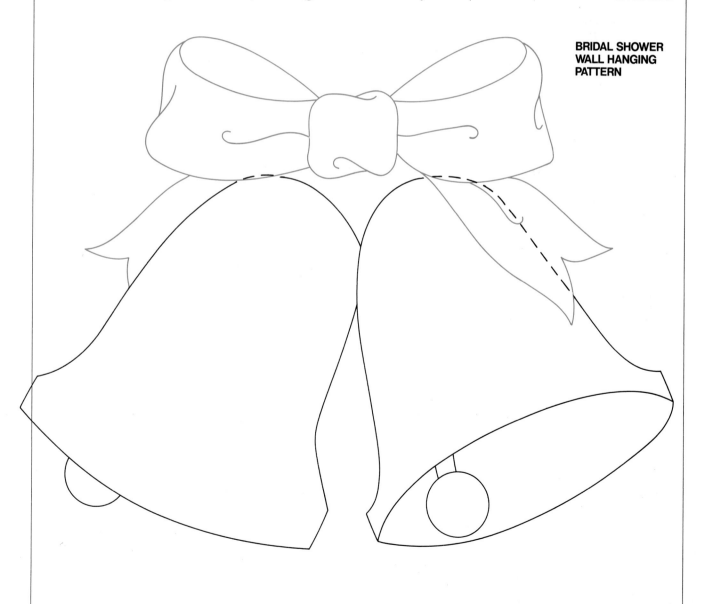

CELEBRATIONS OF FRIENDSHIP

**BRIDAL SHOWER
WALL HANGING
PATTERN**

CHURCH: Position the trunks and treetops; appliqué in place. Pin the steeple in place; appliqué the belfry outline only.

Stitch a yellow bell in the belfry; make a yellow French knot for the clapper (see stitch diagram at *right*). Appliqué a brown roof in place atop the steeple.

Baste a brown door and a blue window in place, then lay the white church fabric on top. Appliqué all pieces in place.

With brown floss, make French knot doorknobs and two outline-stitch birds on the background fabric. For the window, tack a purchased lace motif in place or embroider a flower in the center.

You can embroider the path with brown floss or quilt the outline later.

SHOWER: Appliqué the handle and parasol in place, then the three gift packages. Use 6 inches of each ⅛-inch-wide ribbon to make tiny bows. Tack strips of ribbon onto each package; tack bows on top of packages.

Rainfall can be embroidered with silver thread or it can be quilted later.

continued

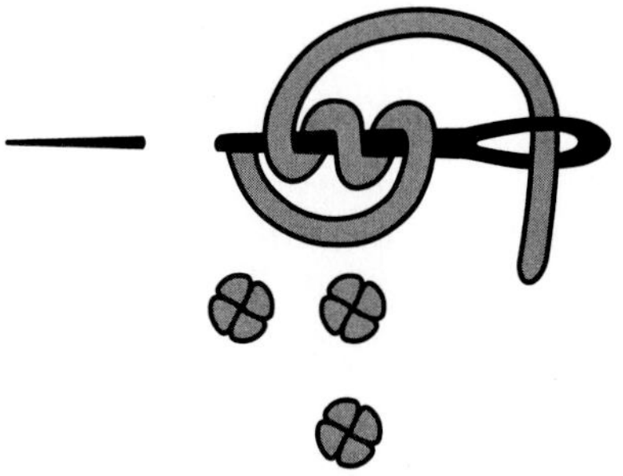

FRENCH KNOT STITCH

BRIDAL SHOWER WALL HANGING PATTERN

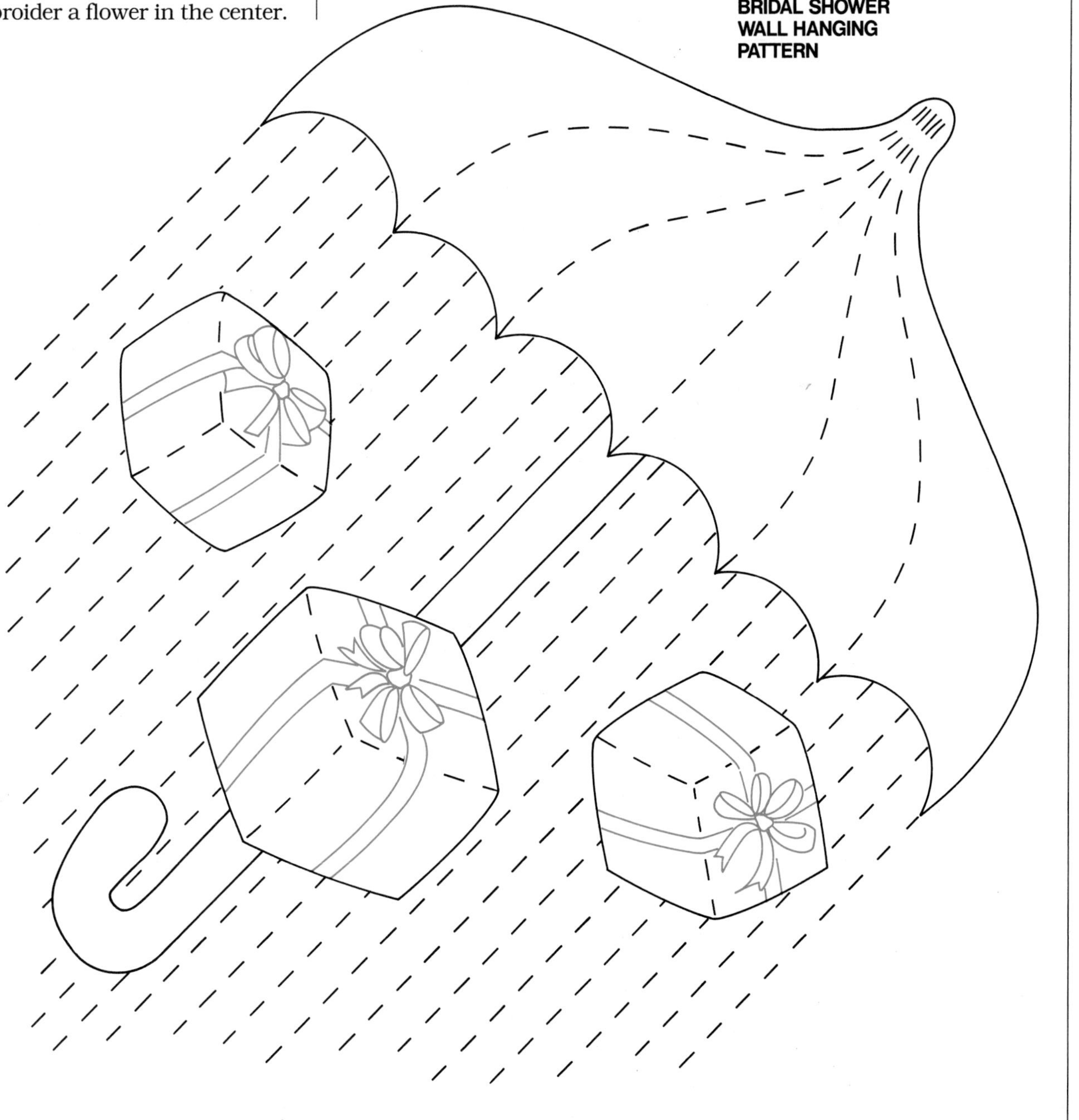

CELEBRATIONS OF FRIENDSHIP

INVITATION: Use a blue permanent marker to write the name and address of the newlywed couple on the envelope appliqué fabric. Stitch the envelope in place, and appliqué a blue stamp in the corner. Appliqué the quill pen. The detail lines in the pen can be quilted later.

WEDDING CAKE: Gather the ½-inch-wide lace to fit the bottom of the cake as shown on the pattern, *opposite*. Baste lace in position on the background square.

Starting at the bottom of the cake, sew each of the four layers in place. Quilting lines define the top and sides of each layer.

Use six strands of the pink embroidery floss to loop festoons of "icing" on each layer of the cake. Tack each loop in place with a ribbon rose. Add a larger ribbon rose to the top of the cake.

ASSEMBLY: Refer to assembly diagram, *opposite,* to join the nine appliquéd blocks, the four solid blocks, and all the setting trian-

gles into five diagonal rows. Add corner triangles to the assembled quilt top. Press seams toward the darker fabric.

Matching centers of the border strips with the edge of the quilt top, sew borders to opposite sides; leave excess fabric at each end for mitering corners. Add borders to remaining sides; miter corners. Press seams toward borders.

**BRIDAL SHOWER
WALL HANGING
PATTERN**

FINISHING: With a nonpermanent marker, draw the quilting design of your choice in the solid setting squares. Our quilt shows a purchased stencil design of a feathered heart, parts of which are repeated in the setting triangles. A floral design was used for the borders. Mark other quilting details, such as the church path.

Layer backing fabric, batting, and quilt top; baste all three layers securely together. Quilt as desired; remove basting threads.

Turn under ½ inch around the border edge; trim the batting and backing ½ inch shorter than the border. Turn the border edge over another ¾ inch; bring the folded edge down over the backing fabric. Hand-sew the folded edge in place on the back.

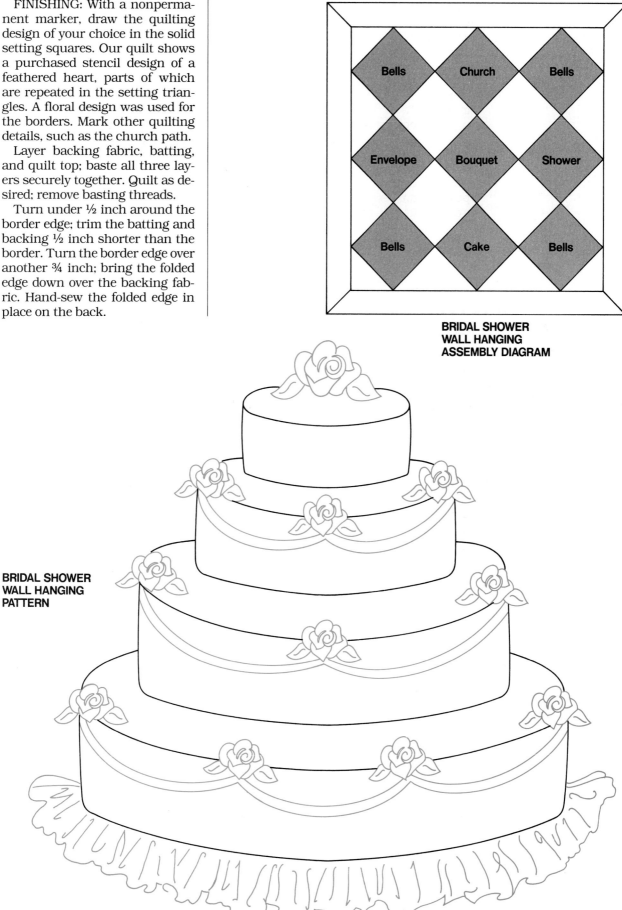

BRIDAL SHOWER WALL HANGING ASSEMBLY DIAGRAM

Bells | Church | Bells
Envelope | Bouquet | Shower
Bells | Cake | Bells

BRIDAL SHOWER WALL HANGING PATTERN

Slumber Party Autograph Sleeping Bag and Pillowcase

Shown on page 61.

The finished (folded) sleeping bag measures 41½x76¼ inches. The pillowcase is 18¾x30 inches.

MATERIALS
4½ yards of pink checked fabric for bag and pillowcase
1⅝ yards of green print fabric for border, binding, and triangle patchwork
⅛ yard *each* of seven fabrics (three dark, four light) for triangle patchwork
4½ yards of muslin for lining
81x96-inches of quilt batting
DMC's Cébélia ecru crochet cotton, Size 5
Large-eyed needle for tying
Permanent marking pen
Pencil and ruler

INSTRUCTIONS
This take-along sleeping bag is constructed flat, then folded and sewn together at the bottom edge. Once someone is in the bag, the side is closed with fabric ties. Tying, instead of quilting, makes this a fast and easy project.

Muslin is recommended for the lining fabric because it provides an unmarked surface for slumber party autographs.

Sleeping bag
CUTTING: *Note:* Measurements given in cutting instructions include ¼-inch seam allowances.

Cut a 3½-inch-wide strip down one side of the pink checked fabric. From this piece, cut eight 3½x20-inch strips for the ties. For the bag, cut two 38x62½-inch pieces from the remaining pink checked fabric.

From the green print fabric, cut eight 4½x39-inch strips for borders. Cut six 2½x42-inch green print strips for the binding.

From the remaining green print and *each* of the seven other patchwork fabrics, cut six 4-inch squares. Cut each square in half *diagonally* to obtain 96 triangles.

Cut the muslin lining fabric into two 2¼-yard lengths.

Save all the remaining fabrics and scraps for the pillowcase.

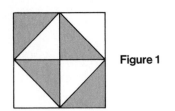

Figure 1

PATCHWORK: Selecting triangles randomly, sew a light triangle to each dark triangle to create 48 triangle-squares. Press seams toward the dark fabrics.

Sew four triangle-squares together to make a 6½-inch block, with the dark and light triangles positioned as shown in Figure 1, *above*. Make 12 blocks.

Join six blocks together to form one 38-inch-long row. Press all seams in one direction. Repeat for the remaining six blocks.

ASSEMBLY: Refer to the assembly diagram of the finished bag, *below,* as you sew.

Sew a pieced border strip onto one 38-inch edge of each of the pink bag pieces. Press the seams toward the pink fabric.

Stitch one strip of border fabric to the top and bottom of each unit. Press seams toward outer border; trim excess length.

Matching the horizontal seam lines, stitch the center seam of the bag. Press seam to one side.

Join the remaining four strips to make two 77½-inch-long side borders. These will be slightly longer than the assembled bag.

Sew one long border strip onto each side of the bag. Press seams toward border; trim excess border fabric. The assembled bag should now measure 83½ inches wide and 76¾ inches long.

6¼"

62"

37½"

SLEEPING BAG ASSEMBLY DIAGRAM

LINING: Seam the two muslin pieces side by side. Press the center seam in one direction.

Layer the lining, batting, and sleeping bag (right side up). Pin or baste the three layers together, starting in the center and working out toward the edges. Baste around the perimeter of the bag, ½ inch from all the edges. The lining and batting are slightly larger than the assembled bag.

TYING: Work on the right side of the sleeping bag.

Thread a large-eyed needle with two 2½-inch lengths of crochet cotton. At one corner of the patchwork border, take a tiny stitch through all three layers.

Remove the needle and pull all four tails of thread even. Tie a knot in the thread on the surface of the sleeping bag.

Position ties across the patchwork border at the corners and the center of each 6-inch block. For the body of the bag, space ties roughly 4 inches apart, starting at one side seam and working across to the opposite side seam.

When tying is complete, trim excess lining and batting; remove basting thread.

SIDE TIES: Fold each 3½x20-inch pink tie strip in half lengthwise, right sides together.

Measure 1¾ inches from the end along the long raw edge. With a pencil, lightly draw a line from this point to the bottom corner, as shown in Figure 2, *below.* This is the sewing line for the tapered point. Machine-stitch on this line, pivot, and continue sewing to the other end.

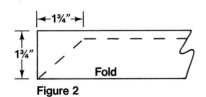

Figure 2

Trim the excess fabric from the tapered end, leaving a ¼-inch seam allowance. Turn the strip right side out through the open end; press.

Make eight side ties.

Position the first tie just below the pieced border. Working on the lining side of the bag, match the raw edge of the tie to the edge of the bag; baste in place.

Position three more ties down the side of the bag approximately 18 inches apart.

Position four ties on the opposite side of the bag, placing them carefully so they will align with those on the first side.

FINISHING: Binding finishes the raw edges at the sides and the top of the sleeping bag. Do not bind the bottom edge.

Seam all the binding strips together; press seams open.

Refer to the tips on page 40 for instructions on applying binding. Start sewing the binding to the bag at the bottom of one side, working up the side, across the top, and down the length of the opposite side.

Fold the bag in half lengthwise, right sides together. Seam the bottom raw edges together to enclose the foot of the bag.

Pillowcase

Note: Desired size may vary depending upon the pillow size. If the pillow is not standard, alter cutting instructions accordingly.

CUTTING: Cut a 8½x38-inch piece of green print border fabric and one 25½x38-inch piece of pink checked fabric.

From the remaining patchwork fabrics, cut twelve 4-inch squares (six dark fabric and six light fabric). Cut each square in half *diagonally* to obtain 24 triangles.

ASSEMBLY: Refer to the diagram of the finished pillowcase, *below,* as you sew.

Sewing light and dark triangles together in pairs, make 12 triangle-squares; press the seam allowances toward the dark fabrics. Seam squares together to form a 38-inch-long border.

Sew the pieced border onto the 38-inch pillowcase fabric. Press seam toward the patchwork.

Sew the 8½x38-inch strip of green print fabric onto the remaining edge of the pieced border. Press the seam away from the patchwork. Press under ¼ inch on the remaining long edge of the green border fabric.

Fold the border fabric over to the back, wrong sides together. Bring the folded edge down to the bottom seamline of the patchwork, covering the raw edges of the seam allowance. Hand-stitch the folded edge of the border fabric in place at the seamline.

With right sides together, machine-stitch the bottom and side seams of the pillowcase. Turn pillowcase right side out and press.

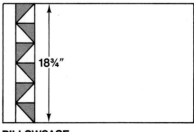

PILLOWCASE ASSEMBLY DIAGRAM

Stadium Blanket And Pillows

Shown on page 62.

The finished blanket measures approximately 70 inches square. The pillows are 16x16x2 inches.

MATERIALS
Note: Yardage is given for 72-inch-wide felt.

For the stadium blanket
1⅜ yards of blue felt
1 yard of yellow felt
⅝ yard *each* of orange felt and green felt
⅜ yard of maroon felt
2 yards of blue felt for backing
Iron-on interfacing
72-inch square of quilt batting
School pennants, awards, letters, pins, medallions, buttons, T-shirts, iron-on letters and motifs
Graph paper and pencil
Optional: water erasable marking pen, embroidery floss, permanent marking pen, invisible thread

For two stadium pillows
⅔ yard of blue felt
¼ yard of orange felt
⅛ yard of yellow felt
Two 16x16x2-inch foam squares or polyester stuffing

INSTRUCTIONS
DECORATING TIPS: A T-shirt shop can be a wonderful source of reasonably priced motifs for your personalized stadium blanket.

In addition to names and mascots of area schools, these shops often carry a wide range of usable slogans and letters. These might include words (such as "Class of 91") or symbols (such as Greek letters for fraternities and sororities) that can be pressed directly onto felt blocks.

If you purchase words or letters at a T-shirt shop, have them ironed onto a piece of white felt and trimmed so that ¼ inch of the white felt shows around each letter (for example, the words "Go, Fight, Win" on our blanket).

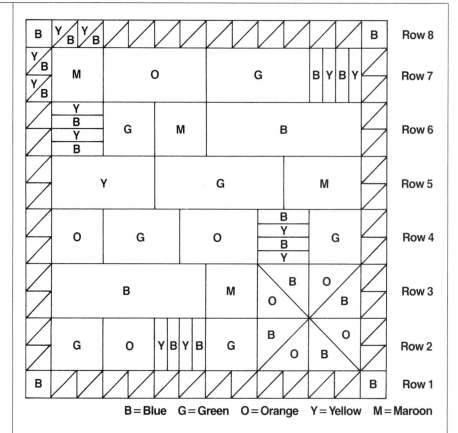

B = Blue   G = Green   O = Orange   Y = Yellow   M = Maroon

To have autographs on some blocks, write or embroider them before the blanket is assembled. Friends, teammates, and family members can sign the felt blocks using either a permanent marker or a water-erasable marking pen. If you like, you can then outline-stitch the autographs using 12 plies of embroidery floss. (See the stitch diagram on page 41.)

To use an old T-shirt logo, press iron-on interfacing to the wrong side of the shirt. Cut out the logo, then tack it onto the felt.

You may wish to use only two or three colors of felt for your blanket rather than the five colors used on our blanket. If so, map out the color placement before beginning and adjust yardage accordingly.

Stadium blanket
CUTTING: The blanket assembly diagram, *above,* shows the block configurations used for the blanket pictured on page 62. Use this pattern to make your blanket or plan your own.

Each border block is a finished size of 5 inches square. All other blocks are 10 inches deep. The width is a multiple of 5 inches; for example, the orange and green rectangles in Row 7 are as wide as four border squares, or 20 inches.

In the blue and yellow striped blocks, each stripe has a finished size of 2½x10 inches.

Draw pattern squares, rectangles, and triangles onto graph paper; add ½-inch seam allowances. Cut out all felt pieces.

ASSEMBLY: Use ½-inch seam allowances throughout.

Anything that is to be ironed on should be attached before any of the pieces are sewn together.

Sew small yellow and blue triangles together to form blocks for the outer border. Sew large orange and blue triangles together to form blocks for rows 2 and 3.

For striped squares, sew two blue and two yellow strips together, alternating colors. Make four striped squares for rows 2, 4, 6, and 7.

Stitch all the blocks together into eight rows, following the assembly diagram or your own plan. Sew the rows together.

Layer blanket front and back with right sides together; lay batting on top. Carefully baste layers together. Stitch a ½-inch seam around the entire perimeter of the blanket, leaving a 10-inch opening on one side.

Trim the batting close to the seam; trim corners. Turn blanket right side out; press edges lightly. Slip-stitch opening closed.

Use invisible thread, embroidery floss, yarn, or buttons to "tie" through all layers at the corners of each block. Tack pennants, letters, motifs, and any other memorabilia in place.

If the blanket is to be used as a wall hanging, sew or pin buttons, awards, and other medallions in place. If it is to be used as a coverlet, omit pins for safety reasons.

Stadium pillows

CUTTING: From the blue felt, cut two 17-inch squares for pillow backs.

From the remaining blue felt, cut two 3x69-inch strips for the sides, and eight 3x9-inch strips. Cut eight more 3x9-inch strips from the yellow felt.

Draw an 8-inch square on the graph paper. Divide the square in half diagonally. Add ½-inch seam allowances around one triangle to make a triangle pattern.

Use this pattern to cut four triangles from both the blue and the orange felt.

PIECING: Alternating blue and yellow strips, sew four 3x9-inch strips into a 9-inch square. Make three more striped blocks. Join blocks into a 17-inch square.

Sew one blue and one orange triangle together along long sides, forming a 9-inch square. Make three more triangle-squares. Join blocks into a 17-inch square.

PILLOW ASSEMBLY: Starting at the center of any side, sew the side piece around pieced top. Allow ample fabric at corners and leave a ½-inch seam allowance free on both short ends. Seam short ends together.

Sew side piece to the pillow back, leaving a 4-inch opening in one side. Turn pillow to right side. Insert foam form or stuffing, then slip-stitch opening closed.

HEARTSTRINGS CRIB QUILT PATTERN

Heartstrings Crib Quilt

Pictured on page 63.

The finished crib quilt measures 38x46 inches. Each of the appliqué blocks is 8 inches square.

MATERIALS:
½ yard *each* of white print and blue print fabrics
⅜ yard *each* of yellow dot, yellow print, green solid, and purple solid fabrics
⅛ yard of red mini dot
1½ yards of backing fabric
1½ yards of quilt batting
Polyester filling
¼ yard of paper-backed fusible webbing
⅛ yard *each* of ⅜-inch-wide and 1-inch-wide grosgrain ribbons in green, blue, red, and purple
18 inches narrow string
Green embroidery floss and needle
Nonpermanent fabric marker
Acrylic ruler
Rotary cutter and mat

INSTRUCTIONS
Instructions are for machine-appliqué, except for the stuffed balloon hearts. If you prefer to appliqué by hand, add seam allowances to each part of the animal and cut all pieces individually. Do not apply fusible webbing to pieces cut for hand appliqué.

CUTTING: Save all scrap fabrics for the checkerboard.

From yellow print fabric, cut two 2½x32½-inch borders and two 2½x39½-inch borders.

From both green and purple fabrics, cut one 7x42-inch strip. Cut each of these strips into six-teen 2½x7-inch sashing strips. Cut eight 2½-inch squares from remaining purple and green fabrics for sashing corners.

From the blue print fabric, cut four 8½-inch squares across the width of the fabric. Cut two 1½x38½-inch blue border strips.

From the remaining blue fabric, cut four 1½-inch-wide strips long enough to piece together two 46½-inch-long border strips.

From the white print fabric, cut three 2½x30-inch strips for the checkerboard. From the remainder, cut eight 6¼-inch squares. Cut each of these squares in half *diagonally* to obtain 16 triangles.

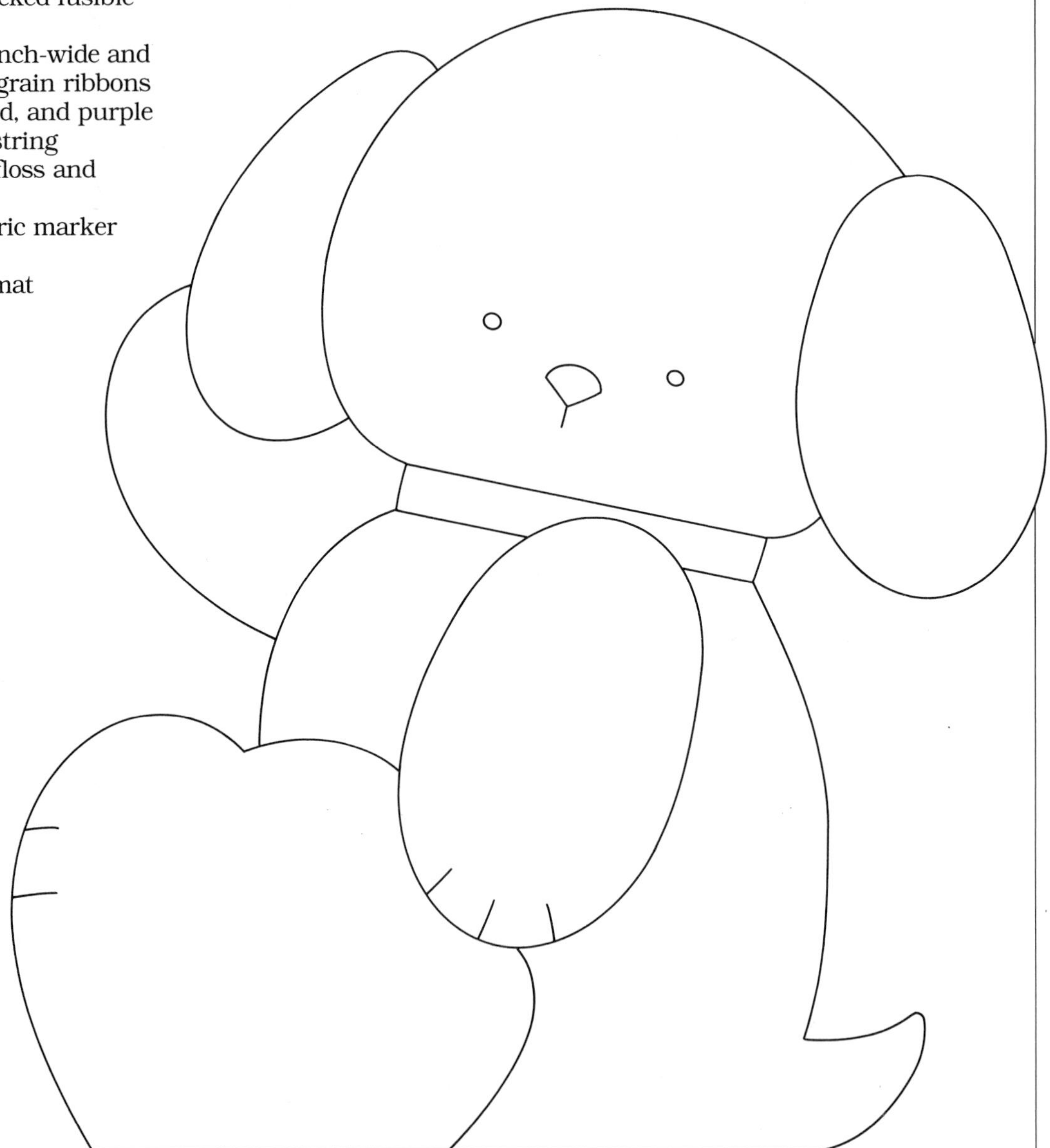

**HEARTSTRINGS
CRIB QUILT
PATTERN**

From the red fabric, cut four 2½-inch squares for the border corners. Adding a ¼-inch seam allowance to the pattern, *left,* cut eight red balloon hearts.

From the yellow dot fabric, cut one strip 5x44 inches. From this strip, cut eight 4⅞-inch squares and four 1½-inch squares. Cut each of the larger squares in half *diagonally* to obtain 16 triangles.
continued

HEARTSTRINGS CRIB QUILT PATTERN

PREPARING THE APPLIQUÉ: Trace the animal shapes and all detail lines from the patterns on pages 75–77 and *opposite* onto the *right* side of the remaining yellow dot fabric. For machine-appliqué, trace each animal body as one piece; only the arm that overlaps the neck ribbon is traced separately. Do not cut pieces yet.

Apply fusible webbing to the *wrong* side of each appliqué. Cut out the shapes, adding ¼ inch only to the bottom edge of each body piece.

Align the bottom edge of one animal body with one edge of a blue print square, centering the body in the square. Pin or baste a ⅜-inch-wide ribbon in place at the neckline, then position the top arm piece of the animal.

Fuse the appliqué fabrics onto the blue print fabric.

APPLIQUÉ BLOCKS: Using a tight, narrow zig-zag stitch, machine-appliqué around each animal shape. Be sure to catch the ribbon in the neckline stitching to secure the collar. Do not stitch the bottom edge of the body.

As you sew around the outstretched paw, insert a ½-inch-long piece of string at the bottom and a 3½-inch-long string at the top so that one end of each string piece is caught in the stitching.

Details such as the outline of a leg or the puppy's ears can be filled in with a line of stitching.

Complete all four appliqués.

With natural-colored thread or monofilament, couch the longer strings onto the background fabric. Let the short strings dangle.

Use six strands of embroidery floss to make French knots for eyes and paw pads; satin-stitch

the noses. Use three strands to outline-stitch the mouths. (See stitch diagrams on page 41.)

Sew white triangles onto opposite sides of each blue square; press seams toward blue fabric. Sew white triangles onto remaining sides of the squares.

CORNER UNITS: Sew a green sashing strip onto one short leg of a yellow dot triangle.

Sew a purple square onto one end of a green sashing strip; sew this pieced strip onto the other leg of the yellow triangle. Both green strips will extend slightly beyond the yellow triangle.

Align the edge of the ruler with the hypotenuse of the triangle; use a rotary cutter to trim the excess sashing. The resulting corner unit is a right-angle triangle.

Make eight corner units with green sashing and eight corner units with purple sashing. Press seams toward sashing.

Sew four same-colored corners onto each appliqué square, sewing opposite sides of the square first, then the remaining sides. Press seams toward sashing.

ASSEMBLY: Sew the finished 16½-inch blocks together in two rows of two squares each. Join the rows by stitching the center seam. Press seams to one side.

Cut thirty-two 2½-inch squares from the three remaining white print strips. Cut 32 more 2½-inch squares from scraps of the colored fabrics.

Join one white square to each colored square; press the seams toward the colored fabrics. Sew the squares into two checkerboard strips of 16 pairs each, referring to the assembly diagram, *left*. Press seams in one direction.

Sew one checkerboard strip to the top edge of the quilt. Press seam away from checkerboard. Repeat at the bottom edge.

Sew the shorter yellow border strips to top and bottom edges of the quilt. Sew a red corner square to each end of the long border strips. Matching seam lines, sew borders to sides. Add the outer blue borders and yellow corner squares in the same manner.

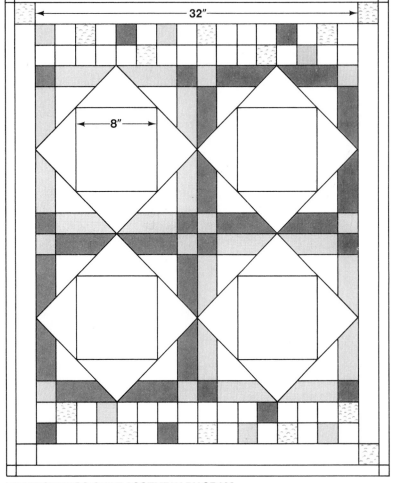

32"

8"

HEARTSTRINGS QUILT ASSEMBLY DIAGRAM

QUILTING AND BINDING: Layer batting, backing fabric, and top; baste securely. Quilt as desired, by hand or by machine.

The quilt shown on page 63 is machine-quilted "in the ditch," or atop seam lines, around the blue squares, white triangles, sashing, and yellow border. Diagonal lines quilted across the checkerboard squares extend into the border.

When the quilting is complete, remove the basting threads. Trim the batting even with the quilt top, but not the backing.

You can make separate binding if you prefer (see page 40); our quilt is bound with the backing fabric turned to the front. For this method, trim the backing fabric to within ¾ inch of the quilt edge.

Press under a generous ¼-inch hem on the edges of the backing. Turn backing fabric over the quilt edge to the top; hand- or machine-stitch folded edge in place on top.

FINISHING TOUCHES: Make a small slit in the center of one red heart piece. Sew the slit heart to another heart piece, right sides together, stitching all around. Clip curves and points; turn right side out through the slit; press.

Use an unsharpened pencil or some other tool to poke little bits of stuffing into the heart. When stuffed, whipstitch the slit closed.

Make four balloon hearts.

Tack the puffy heart balloons in place at the top of each animal's string. The heart should straddle the seam line between the blue and white fabrics.

Cut a 2-inch length of wide ribbon for each bow tie. In the center of each piece, hand-stitch a gathering thread across the 1-inch width of the ribbon. Pull on the thread to gather up the ribbon; wrap thread tightly around ribbon to secure gathers. Tack bows in place on the quilt top.

**HEARTSTRINGS
CRIB QUILT
PATTERN**

ACKNOWLEDGMENTS

We would like to extend our thanks to the following designers who contributed projects to this book.

Marina Anderson—63

Backstreet Designs—46
P.O. Box 213
Athens, AL 35611

Marilyn Ginsburg—58-59

Vicky Haider—12-13

Lynette Jensen—47, 61

Long Island Quilters'
    Society, Inc.—8

Ann Nunemacher—60

Sally Paul—48, 49

Susan Abbie Ray—62

Marcia Shoemaker—4-5

Patricia Wilens—44-45

We would like to thank the following people whose technical skills are greatly appreciated.

Marianne Fons

Judy Pletcher

Elizabeth Porter

Leone Rusch

Marcia Shoemaker

Margaret Sindelar

Judith Veeder

A special thank-you is extended to the following persons who graciously loaned us antiques or otherwise assisted in the production of this book.

Brunnier Gallery
Iowa State University
Ames, IA 50011

Buckboard Antiques & Quilts
Judy Howard
1411 N. May
Oklahoma City, OK 73107

Carol Dahlstrom

Peggy Freylack

Glendora Hutson

Marti and Dick Michell

Holly Swartzbaugh
    and Jack Vermie

Sara Jane Treinen

We also are pleased to acknowledge the following photographers whose talents and technical skills contributed much to this book.

George Ceolla—9

Hopkins Associates—17-23;
    30-31; 42-43; 58-61

Scott Little—4-5; 12-13; 24-29;
    32, 36, 44-49; 63

Perry Struse—8

Dean Tanner—7

If you have comments or questions regarding this book, please write to the editors at:

BETTER HOMES AND
GARDENS® CRAFT BOOKS
1716 Locust Street, No. 352
Des Moines, IA 50336

Have BETTER HOMES AND
GARDENS® magazine delivered
to your door. For information,
write to:
MR. ROBERT AUSTIN
P.O. BOX 4536
DES MOINES, IA 50336